Christian Williams was born and raised in a small town of South Wales called Merthyr Tydfil. He grew up without a dad in his life, or a father figure. His 29-year-old father passed away in a tragic fire when he was just six years old. This death was one of so many that would continue to follow.

Christian had a troubled time right up until he was 15 years old, and that is when he found his calling. He vented all his frustration, anger, pain, and confusion in the weights room and that is where he discovered his true self. He found a way to turn all that negative energy into a positive outcome. Which helped him develop a physique that would go on to win multi bodybuilding championships and take him into a career that would change the lives of so many other people.

He got over his fear of speaking in public and now he is an international public speaker who also leads a team of other speakers all seeking to change the world through the power of voice. He invests much of his time working on himself, his body, mind, and spirit, which he encourages others to do through his charismatic personality.

What he knows, he knows, and what he does not, he doesn't claim. Throughout his life he had experienced many significant times where he had been guided from above, through a spiritual connection.

What he has learnt is that the path to knowing is a lonely one, and it is that way for a good reason.

His father has helped him more in his death than in his life, and has gifted him with the awareness of his presence.

Christian believes that through this life we are just passing for a short time, and we have control of our experience, it is just a matter of choice, so, why not make it the best possible one.

I would like to dedicate this book to my father who has been there even when he wasn't.
He has taught me how to be a man even though it was the hard way. That too I am very thankful for.

Your life was devoted to an art you felt so passionate about. You have passed on that internal desire, drive, and dedication which has helped me in so many ways. I couldn't have written this book without you. In fact, it was you who inspired me to write it after reading your diary thank you for everything I have and everything I don't.

The gift you have given me is the gift of knowing, know thyself.

Young Christian with his father John, and his sister Simone

Christian Williams

START A FIRE!

In Your Heart

AUSTIN MACAULEY PUBLISHERS™
LONDON • CAMBRIDGE • NEW YORK • SHARJAH

Copyright © Christian Williams 2023

The right of Christian Williams to be identified as author of this work has been asserted by the author in accordance with Federal Law No. (7) of U.A.E., Year 2002, Concerning Copyrights and Neighboring Rights.

All rights reserved. No part of this publication may be reproduced, stored in a retrieval system, or transmitted in any form or by any means, electronic, mechanical, photocopying, recording, or otherwise, without the prior permission of the publishers.

Any person who commits any unauthorized act in relation to this publication may be liable to legal prosecution and civil claims for damages.

The age group that matches the content of the books has been classified according to the age classification system issued by the Ministry of Culture and Youth.

ISBN – 9789948789345 – (Paperback)
ISBN – 9789948789352 – (E-Book)

Application Number: MC-10-01-4930888
Age Classification: E

Printer Name: iPrint Global Ltd
Printer Address: Witchford, England

First Published 2023
AUSTIN MACAULEY PUBLISHERS F.Z.E.
Sharjah Publishing City
P.O. Box [519201]
Sharjah, U.A.E.
www.austinmacauley.ae
+971 655 95 202

To my amazing mother, Elaine Williams. Wow, I don't believe I have enough paper to explain how thankful I am for having been born into your loving arms. You were a mum, a dad, a teacher, and a friend to me, and still are. Seeing the effort, you have put in to support me, finding a way when there was none, has given me the work ethic, the willpower, and the commitment to my family. I am internally grateful for the love you have given me and always believing in me. You are the toughest person I know; I owe my life to you.

To my beautiful wife, Carly Williams. You are my anchor; you are my Yin; you balance me perfectly; you keep me grounded; you nurture me and help me grow. Thank you for always supporting me even when you didn't understand why. Your loyalty and your adoration towards me is what makes me feel like I am enough just the way I am. I love you; I always did and I always will.

Simone Williams, my big sister, but little one too. You have always been there for me through thick and thin. You are my star sent from above, guiding me through the dark night, always shining light on me, making me trust my intuition and intentions.

Thank you for always being there, for introducing me to Darren and your sweet angels, and for loving me unconditionally.

I would like to thank everyone I have mentioned in this book: my close friends and distant ones, mentors, coaches, all my family and friends as well as my clients and the people I have met along the way. You have individually and collectively shaped me as the man I am today; you are all part of me. Any of my success, the highs and the lows, you have been the connecting bridge to my future and I wouldn't want to change any of the experiences.

And last but not least, this one is for a special someone that has not yet come into my life, but I feel him coming. My son, Clark J. Williams. Your spirit is felt, and you have given me more drive than I thought I could obtain. The context of this book is written to pass to you so that one day if you are in a similar situation, which I am sure you will be, as that is what life is about, you will be able to learn from my emotional experiences and will feel guided through, just like I felt from my father's diary. What you choose to do, how you choose to act, is entirely up to you. That is your choice; it is your life. I am just here to help you reach your definition of success.

Table of Contents

Chapter 1: The Diary	13
Chapter 2: Signs of the Past	27
Chapter 3: My Obsession	39
Chapter 4: The Struggle Is Real	49
Chapter 5: My Intuition	64
Chapter 6: My Queen	76
Chapter 7: The Land of My Father	89
Chapter 8: Facing My Fears	111
Chapter 9: My Therapy	124
Chapter 10: What I Was Seeking Was Seeking Me	138
Chapter 11: The Break	150
Chapter 12: What Will Be Will Be	166
Chapter 13: The Passing of Ages	182

Chapter 1
The Diary

I've woken up in the middle of the ocean in a cabin standing far in the sea. I hear the sound of the waves crashing against the wooden frame that surrounds this peaceful sanctuary, I lay lifted high into the clean mystical air by the pillars that secure me there.

The sun beams onto the glass of the sliding doors that seal the calmness outside but let's just enough light in to bring me out of a pleasant dream and into the beautiful world I was birthed into.

I feel the warmth of my blood running smoothly through my veins. My breath fills my lungs as my eyes open slowly and glare upon the distance to what many only see in their dream or pray to see.

Is this a dream? It feels like paradise.

Is it? It could be.

I see miles of endless ripples carrying water from as far back as my eyes can reach, and today my eyes seem so clear; I can see further than yesterday, but still the ocean expands far beyond.

I step outside the bed and feel the wooden ground below me. I grip the old, solid paving that's beneath me. It secures my blessings. I take a moment to appreciate my gifted senses and awareness of where I am today.

I am alone but I know I am not, I am spiritually connected, and the presence of another is felt. I gently walk toward the doors and slide them open. I feel the light hit my rested soul and spark my presence. I admire where I am and reminisce on where I have been, which brings a gentle smile to my face as my awareness shifts into the knowledge of what this day will lead to.

I take a few steps forward and sit outside in a perfect position to gaze upon the breathtaking view from this incredible Treasure Island.

It's a place where I will discover more, more about myself, my purpose, and my true desires. Today is the beginning of the end, and I feel a sense of confidence as if I have prepared for it.

I feel my surrounding like I am one, I am the ocean, the air; I am connected to everything.

I am truly present in the now and I feel the calm knowledge of knowing. The breeze from the ocean before me carries a warm message of hope to my delicate skin.

The waves carry along the glaring reflection of the sun, that as woken to, like the God of us all that brings us to this reality, this consciousness and with it carries joy and happiness. The air flows into my lungs as I take a slow but deep breath. I hold it for a minute before setting it free, releasing the tension I felt and replacing it with the gratitude I feel for my waking here today and the gift to experience all this glory.

I admire the journey that has passed and the one that lies ahead.

Today is a day I will never forget, that's for sure.

Today is the bridge to another day. I feel more alive than ever, confident, and willing.

Today is a special day, one I have been preparing for most of my life, one that I will remember for longer than the time I waited.

Today is a day I knew I would feel this way. It's the 9th of May, and today is the anniversary of my father's death.

John Kaler, my dad, died at the age of 29, in a tragic fire 26 years ago.

He is a man that has guided me, encouraged me, and supported me to this day.

He has taught me many life's lessons. He is a man that I know I will see again and one that I have always felt near.

My father has had a massive influence in my life. He has passed on the light to shine onto those around.

Our relationship was also short-lived, but he was still able to give me so much knowledge, experience, and wisdom. He taught me from his lessons and guided me from above.

He died when I was just six years old. He separated from my mother when I was still being pushed in a pram.

The separation was a difficult one filled with pain, anger, confusion, and frustration, at least that's what I am told.

My father had to fight for custody to see me, which he was gracefully granted for some time. I would go with him twice a week I believe, but never overnight, just a few hours. One night, he didn't return me back home at the time agreed. He didn't want to; he wanted more time. The police were involved which led to him losing custody and his right to see me.

I have always felt him with me, his personality shine through me. Like he has been there, seeing all my successes, picking me up whenever I fell down.

Today I am not upset by the reminder of his death. I am celebrating his life, his spirit released into the present for eternity. Today I am celebrating my life and my awareness of his.

I am so grateful for the little time we did spend together and grateful of the lifetime of development I know it will lead to.

Today is a special day. It is an important one. It is a different anniversary, different from the rest. It's one I have been waiting for and for some time, though the thought of today often brought a lot of excitement, anxiety too.

I made the decision to do something today before this day even came and now it is finally here.

Today I will read it, the diary my father wrote and left for me. The diary in which he documented his thoughts, his feelings, his struggles, the hardships he faced, the pain leading right up to his death from three years before it. It has been nested for me, for many curious years.

Before I chose to read it, I had to reach a certain point in my life when I wouldn't be easily influenced; a certain age, the passing of ages, where one life ended and another one began.

I knew I had to be in a mentally stable position, strong enough and ready for this journey I was about to explore. To take a glimpse into the life of my father's.

I have so many questions and I know the answers are there for me in this expression of one's emotions on paper, from someone so close to me yet so far away.

I am now a confident, strong, and powerful man myself. I know my direction, purpose, my calling if you like.

Today I have no fear of anything, let alone what is written or what I will read. I know that it was written to be read, to be read by me, read by me today.

I feel honored to have this opportunity to share past experiences which will spark new ones for me, I'm sure.

I am ready and I am not alone.

The first page from my father's dairy

June 1990

Order out of chaos.

But how?

How can I know?

What can I do?

Have I opened a Pandora's Box?

If so, how can I close it?

Through death?

Or life?

Life seems hopeless.

But there is hope.

God have mercy.

God help, God send down your beloved angels.

Already it is over, they said.

Is it true or what?

What is happening?

They tell me.

This catastrophe.

Or but not really.

Have they gone mad?

Or is it me?

As I began to read, I could see that my father had questions of his own that he was searching answers for. Maybe that's what keeps his quest alive? Hopefully he would have found them before his life ended in the fire, he died three years after he began writing his diary.

My father was a very expressive person, he was a poet; singer , musician; he was an extremely gifted artist; he had so much talent, drive, ambition, I guess he chose not to verbally share all his pain and struggles, instead choosing other methods: writing, singing, playing the guitar, and painting. That's why I know this diary will be a tough read and record so many unspoken truths of upsetting memories all documented over pages of handwritten stories that led to his grave.

The first few pages made my throat go dry instantly, like I was being strangled, trying to cry for help, but I quickly realized that I was feeling the emotions he experienced, the suffering he was going through, which could be the reason he waited this long to pass me the messages.

Now I understand more.

Did I choose the right time?

Or was this time chosen for me?

Was I being led from above, guided to this moment, to this position in life? Has it been waiting for me to reach this point?

Like I have been waiting?

Was it always part of the puzzle, my puzzle, my journey?

Is this the reason I am now this adaptive to anything life throws?

Am I reading it today because I am ready?

Or is it ready for me to read it today?

Regardless of the questions this brings, and I am sure it will bring more as I turn each page and strip back the layers. I can withstand any situation and I welcome all of them too. I have gained so much trust in my own ability more so than ever today, my intuition is strong, I know it comes to me with a meaningful purpose.

Today I am reborn, for the first time ever in my life, I feel complete, and confident in myself. I am set free from the pressure I placed on myself for many years, using the excuses that because I lost my father and had no father figure to guide me, I was being a dad to myself. A tough one, too hard and straight, trying to win my own approval! Which sounds crazy, but this is the truth because I am opening up, expressing my imbedded feelings and beliefs without trying. In fact, as I put my hand to this pen, words flow out of my mind as they meet this paper. I too am shocked by this statement, as I have never openly admitted it even to myself. Now I know my father was always guiding me, giving me strength through tough times, helping me become as strong as I am in the now to go forward into what lies before me.

My father has always been there, listening, watching, pushing, and pulling. He is even here now as I express myself so easily, never judging. I never need to win his approval. He supports my choices and allows me to find my own way.

To become a dad of my own one day, to pass on all my wisdom, the guidance and knowledge I have felt and been blessed to receive.

From this incredible sense of love I feel, that flows through me like the ocean below me, it makes we wonder, what must it be like?

I can only imagine how it must feel to have a son of my own. To be a teacher to the most loving and loyal student that is cut from the same cloth. To share stories of life's experiences, the highs and the lows, to pass on the torch and carry the legacy that I am confidently creating! Like I am doing for my dad, sharing his life and achievements through my own.

Maybe that's what his diary was created for, for me to write this book, the inspiration I have to devote the hours needed to share his story with the world and also document mine.

As my mind wonders, I start to see the trails of breadcrumbs leading from my past to this day. Signs and messages planted into my subconscious mind start to make sense and I realize why they were so impacting on my emotions then.

A few days back I was in Bohol, I attended a top 1% event with one of my mentors, J.T. Foxx, the world's number-one wealth-and-business coach.

The entire event was all about business. How we could strategize a plan for the rest of 2019 leading into 2020 and help grow my business that was driven by the sole purpose, and soul's purpose, sign up more clients, scale up fast, so more people are transformed, which will positively improve more people's lives.

The event was exclusive to clients of J.T., the ones that were willing to pay a high-ticket price. I was one of around 15 other entrepreneurs and businesses owners. Many were very successful and reaching new heights in their career. Some with startups, but we all had one thing in common besides the quest, we wanted to be the best we could be, to take our businesses to new heights. We also seem to have similar challenges, struggles and barriers that were stopping us from getting to the next level in our life, although all our businesses were different.

We discussed our ideas openly and confidently in a group and got coached one-on-one by the Simon Cowell of business coaching himself, which was extremely intense, but designed to learn from each other, grow individually but also together.

Many of the others were highly successful, and a lot senior to me, they had businesses for many years and had been a part of the J.T. family-coaching team for some time, which was so encouraging to see. It was a very influential trip, one that I knew would create financial movement, improve my business intelligence, help me grow inside out!

We spent five days at a holiday resort that was booked out for only us. We got to know each other very well, well enough to feel comfortable discussing not just our businesses but our personal lives too.

One guy I met left me with many useful attributes to take forward. He was worth over 500 million dollars. He had businesses all around and had done business with very globally recognized men like Tony Robbins and Grant Cardon, so he was speaking with authority but in such a calm and inviting way. He was quite a character too, funny and very down to earth. He was 50 years old but still had a schoolboy charm even though he was obviously highly successful, very educated, and extremely driven. There was a side to John I was not too drawn into though, that was his ego-driven side, although deep down I knew it was my own ego pulling me back, my competitive side acting defensive, my animal instinct feeling threatened by another alpha male, one that had more power and authority than I did. John offered me so much great advice in business, in life, in relationships, in fact anything I asked him he was happy to help. Sometimes I didn't ask, and he was still eager to give and I sensed he knew I needed it. He took a liking to me, maybe he saw a reflection of his younger self. There was a reason why we met, like there is a reason for every encounter and event. No matter how big or small, everything is positioned perfectly in place at precisely the right time in order to progress, like the diary I had waiting for the right timing.

One night we were having dinner, and John was having a few glasses of red wine as he did most nights. He spoke about his first and only child who was one year old, his baby boy. He clearly adored him because his eyes lit up whenever he talked about him. I could feel the love-enriched vibrations flourish out of him and be absorbed by many souls willing-to-listen, the energy was infections and incredible to observe. John told us why he did not have a child until the age of 50. He said he was so driven and focused that no woman could hold him down long enough or keep him grounded, the fact that having a child was something he never even considered as he pushed forward on his path. He confessed that the thought of having a distraction from his goal was something he didn't need. He was a man on a mission and nothing or nobody would hold him back.

But yet he spoke about his son with so much passion and love, it was a joy to listen to and watch his body change before us. He finished telling us how amazingly intelligent he was and how much happiness he brought, how he now feels successful.

I was intrigued by this because I was thinking exactly the same as he did when he was younger, like a child would hold me back from achieving my goals and ambitions. I asked John if I could ask him a personal question, one in front of around ten other inspired listeners.

"Ask me anything, buddy," John confidently answered as he picked up his wine glass and took another sip. I asked him that if he had his son back 20 years ago, did he think he would have achieved the same level of success in his businesses and have the financial freedom he had now? Or would having a son to take care of, play with, teach, force him to take his foot off the gas a little, back off from putting in so many hours into building an empire and pursuing his wildest dreams.

He looked at me straight in my eye, his gaze connected with me and locked me in, like he was talking to the depth of my subconscious mind, and he said, "Nothing would have stopped me back then, buddy."

He quickly added, "There was no turning that drive off." Then a grin came on his serious face and a little laugh which was followed by a few seconds of a pause, then he continued, "In fact, if I had my son back then, I would have had even more drive, more purpose, more reason, more success."

He spoke about how having a son has shaped his life for the better, that he values his time more now so he works more proactively, not just actively. He charges more for his time because now it's far more important. Every minute is more precious and there is a price for his distance away from his son.

Hearing John speak with this much clarity about having a son, hearing this self-made millionaire talk with so much passion and love was so inspiring to me, even more so than all the other stories he told about his success in business or even all the advice he gave me up until this point. This was more impactful and more useful for me moving forward into the rest of my life as I was 20 years younger than John, well, almost, and this was a powerful message.

My father, John Kaler, would have been around John's age if he was still here today, and knowing the love my father had for me, how successful he was at such a young age, how driven and passionate he was, if he was here today, tonight, and I asked him the same question, would he have answered it the same way? The probability is high and it left a powerful impression in my core of awareness.

That night, I pondered and wondered how it must feel to have a son, to watch him grow into a boy and then into a man, to answer these questions when he reached the same point in your life where you went through the same confused states of blindness, not knowing where to turn or what direction to push toward. A beautiful journey, the circle of life, from one being to the next, growing old with your son growing beside you. This was a very happy experience to envision and an exciting moment to live.

I then started thinking how it must feel to have my son taken away from me, to fight for custody to see him only a few hours a week, and how it must feel if my life ended before I had the chance to teach him to fight for his rights, before he became a mature boy, a young man, needing a little help solve the puzzles he will meet, answer the questions of confusion, like the one I asked. I thought about my father and how he passed when I was just six years old, but I didn't have any sympathy for me growing up without a dad because I learnt my way and I was guided in many ways too, but I did think about him not being a part of it or at least experience it with me in the flesh. I know if I have a son, I would fight for him until my death and, even after that, I would find a way to still fight, to do everything in my power to be there when he needed me the most. If there was a way to stay around, I would find it, so I can guide him through the struggles he will face, the ones I faced.

From what many people have told me, from what I have also witnessed, I am very much like my dad. I carry many of his visual features and personality characteristics, so I know he would have felt exactly the same; he would not have left. He would have fought; he would still be fighting now. He would never have left; he is still here now; he is always near. I know that much because I feel his presence close to me, I feel it like a beat in my heart. So close, like a whisper in my ear, a shiver down my arms, the push in the right direction when I need it, and the intuitive gut feeling that warns me of something that's not good.

The diary

Dear Lord, I am now 29 years of age.

For one year, help me to stay put and learn your gospel well so that when I'm 30, I can go and follow in your steps, traveling from place to place and sharing your gospel. Dear Lord, I hope that you will guide me in achieving this.

First, though, I need time for my body to heal. I'll need to be strong-minded by that time.

I don't want to be a false one but true and straight.

Chapter 2
Signs of the Past

The beautiful magical day continues here on this Island. I leave my wooded, suspended cabin and proceed with my morning rituals that I do everywhere I go. I start with a power walk to get the blood moving, to appreciate being alive, to smell the fresh air, stimulate my metabolism, help my digestion start moving waste around my colon, and prepare for the food that follows, but the difference today is the location and the breathtaking views. As I charge up the pathways of flowers and greenery that lead to mountain peaks, I keep my mind in silence and clear my thoughts of anything past to absorb the present, I then proceed with repeating the series of affirmations I always do each morning. I speak out loud words of meaning, and programming, self-love, self-respect, happiness, gratitude, how great I am, how empowered I am, how I am impacting others positively. I say this with confidence and I feel it in my body with the warm rushing flows of joy that follow and run through me. After 30 minutes, I find a quiet spot to sit, cross my legs, close my eyes, and I start to pray. What's ironic is that I don't even know who I'm praying to, it's not to a God, for a religion; to anything specific at this point in my understanding, but I know my prayers are being listened to and someone or something is picking it up for sure. I never questioned this either, never had any doubt, I just trusted what I felt! I pray with no expectations, or expect anything in return. I usually pray for others because I want others to feel as positive as I do about life and find the strength, courage and faith to get through anything life throws and it throws a lot.

Although I don't understand much more than what I see at this point, I know that one day I will be able to see more, and everything will make far more sense to my being. One day I will have all the answers to my questions and that day will be the day I am ready to leave this life. But in the present, it's not important, what is, is that I share my gift, my love, the light, my passion, the desire, and I fulfil my ambition to help as many people as I can feel as positive as I do, as strong as I do, so those that have the desire but lack the self-belief receive what they need to follow their passion too and become the best version of themselves.

My morning prayer

Dear Lord, Guider, Father,

Thank you for this given day, for placing me in this surrounding, placing everything perfectly in place for me to experience.

Thank you for the struggles I have faced, for the struggles that are still to come, for I know they will make me stronger and become a better man.

I am privileged with this gift that I have been given and promise to share.

I will lead by an example to those that wish to follow, and those that don't yet, I will encourage to do so when the time is right for them through my positive actions.

Send my love across the oceans to all my loved ones that are no longer within physical touch, but through my powerful spirit I know they will be reached and my love will be felt.

For my life has meaning, for that I am sure to give and send a piece of my heart across this ocean and connect with theirs.

Amen

I am not religious, nor do I follow what is perceived to be the right way to live from a biblical script or preacher, I was never directed to follow someone else or obey others. My mother gave me the freedom to speak and act as I pleased, in restricted boundaries obviously, but she encouraged me to make the right decisions that were for the better of all around me. I choose to pray every day because I feel like I am doing good in a challenging world. I am sending my energy out physically, verbally, emotionally, and spiritually.

It's something I enjoy doing; it makes me feel cleansed, I feel powerful and influential too. To where it goes, to whom I'm praying to, and who carries the message to my loved ones is still a mystery at the moment, but I know it is received, this I feel, my messages are being connected to many, somehow. Again, it's my intuitive side I have always had and been aware of. It's this knowledge that made me feel different all my life, my own unique understanding of my world, my creation, and my journey.

On this anniversary of my father's death, this beautiful day of celebration and movement evolves, and I feel so much joy, it's like I'm a magnet attracting vibrations around: sounds, friction, thoughts. I feel so connected, receiving so many incredible messages of thanks from those I have been fortunate enough to meet along my journey that have touched and been touched, those encouraged to impact, take risks, to push their career and take a leap of trust that will lead to progression, gaining confidence and faith, to find more appreciation and respect.

Through my gift of seeing the positive vibes in every situation, I have confidently encouraged so many people to go after their goal, to chase dreams, to face fear and feel no fear at all. I have fueled many into the direction they wanted to go but only wished to go and never pursued it. With my amplified love and care, I have been able to give support even when I was not there in person; I was able to connect with them deeply.

Today, everything has grown. My skill, my ability, my gifts, the tools I have gathered that will allow me to work harder and more productively, my spiritual belief, my knowing, my purpose, I have excelled to new levels of feelings.

Today I am empowered, complete, aligned, content, confident, excited, ready to take my life to the next step. I want to stay in this moment I am in here today. It has lifted me up and I feel a joy I have never felt. I am at peace with the struggles I have faced and have acceptance for those being a necessary part of my chosen path, the path that felt chosen for me, but by whom I am yet to discover.

I explore this magical island with a dear friend of mine, one that has come into my life quite recently but one that I have connected with ease, without trying. We seemed to get on and know each other long before we actually did. She is like a friend I have had for years, who seems to understand me like I seem to understand her too. Although I never told her that this day was so important to me, she somehow knew and knew it would bring a lot of emotions but only pleasant ones. The odds that I would be waking up on the day of the anniversary of my father's death with so good energy around me was something I never considered. Maybe that is why I procrastinated for so long to read his diary, maybe that is another lesson for me, and for you, that fear is not real, it only lives in the mind and it should not be the reason to stop us taking action!

Or maybe if it wasn't for this moment, the places I have been, the people I have in my life, I would not be feeling this way and it would not be the right time to explore the expression of one's self that is the closest to heart.

This place is very special and a special place to many, it is a place where you feel your being breaking out of the shell that carries it, the shell protects it from this aggressive world, well, at least that's what I have experienced here so far on my trip. What a place to celebrate a life, a connection, a presence, one I am lucky to have been a part of, even if it was short-lived, at least in the physical world.

I am blessed to be in a place with so much organic life, bonding together for highs and lows, streams that flow into the sea of possibilities, ripples that emerge everything together and becoming one.

I will always be thankful for my visit and being able to share it with a friend of mine, that has been sharing this experience too. I often called her M. J., Madam Jevily, because she has two personalities. One is a bubbly, like the Duracell rabbit, always laughing and fooling around; so much energy. And the other is straight, no messing around, snappy.

Like a whip she would crack from one end to the other, almost like she had bipolar disorder, but she didn't. I thought it was funny at times and would tease her about it. She is 38 years old but looks ten years younger. Maybe it's because although she is so full of life, wisdom, joy, and happiness, she is also very youthful in her actions and enjoys fun times, connecting with the youth too. She's lived in Dubai for the past 16 years, building a successful business and fulfilling her dreams.

I first met Jevily in 2017 shortly after moving to Dubai to pursue my goals and ambitions, to make a better life for myself than I had back in the Valleys of my hometown Merthyr Tydfil in South Wales, U.K. She was starting up a yoga class and asked if I could help her get it going. Somehow, she recognized I had an interest in yoga and freeing my body as well as mind, although I looked like a tank in size and very muscle-bound, not the typical yoga practitioner, but what I can do is talk to anyone and gain their trust very easily. It's a gift I have, one I only use to encourage others to better themselves by applying themselves in something I believe will do just that. For me it's been bodybuilding or building a better body. Most people want to look a certain way, but they don't do what is needed to achieve, and the truth is that deep down they don't believe they can, so they settle for less and accepted they will always look that way, but I know this is so far from the truth.

The class was targeting men mostly and some women, all of whom who, like me, were into bodybuilding and suffering from the effects of lifting heavy day in day out can lead to.

So, we collaborated, and it was very successful, productive, and funny at times, especially when we were all struggling to get into the simplest poses that normally relaxed the yogis but not us, we were red-faced, sweating, grunting, swearing, we were overdeveloped humans and not built with such elegance. Well, maybe we were, but not how we built other selves to be!

Since then, Jevily and I connected, and we became good friends. We shared many times together, socializing, attending events, enjoying each other's company, for food, shisha, and now on this memorable trip.

We were collaborating business ideas together, which is what led us both to be in the Philippines together in the first place. I was coming here to spend a few days with my business coach, and I was told I could bring a spouse or a business partner, and since we were going in that direction anyway, she was a business partner and we spoke about expanding it, she decided to come along with me.

Of course, there was another woman that I had in mind and only hoped that could come with me and that was my wife, but she didn't want to take the time from her busy schedule, running a salon in Dubai, which was a little sad as I had her in mind when I signed up to go. But when she said she couldn't, I was planning to go alone because I didn't have anyone close to me. Not many people I would/could share this experience and knowledge with. My circle is very small to be honest, but tight. I am very social but often enjoy my own company or the company of a selective few. When I mentioned it to her, she was all in because she saw the benefits too. She said she would come to support me and my business, learn from the best, and take the opportunity that was ahead, but it came with a proposal.

"I will come with you for five days to Bohol, support you, be there for whatever you need from me," she said quite firmly, which was followed by a pause and swift in tonality; it got lighter and softer, "But you have to come with me to Davao so I can visit my family and friends before we fly back," then a smile. It seemed like a fair deal and one we would both benefit from. First few days business and learning, then travel to a place I have wanted to go to for some time and discuss how we can put the plans into action when we returned to Dubai. It was a deal, after I spoke to my wife of course.

The diary

1 June 90

> *Look, it's like this*
>
> *Everything has happened*
>
> *Has been a bad dream*
>
> *A bloody nightmare*
>
> *An overdose of a fog and imagination*
>
> *Or thought of something*
>
> *Dis contact*
>
> *Tomorrow I'll awake*
>
> *And the world will be normal as before*
>
> *And I'll change it in a small way*

Was I hypnotized?
Was I already?
Was I conditioned this?
It's a game?

Once not long ago, I worked hard and enjoyed it too
I was inspired
Now, however, I feel expired
This doesn't worry me as much as all the others (people) who may encounter bad things
The man behind the mirrors and I hate it; there's a past feeling of happiness
People suggest various ideas, but I don't know which way to turn
I am hopeless but there is still hope
If I stop seeing myself as self, maybe that may do something
I get this tunnel vision which narrows down to my mind and my memory disappears

I forget names and places

17 June 90

Woke up this morning, there was a clear blue sky.

I got out of bed and it clouded over.

Am I the one bad apple?

In a barrel of apples?

Am I a maggot?

Amongst a million of ripe fruit

Maggots can turn into butterflies.

Argh, I was a butterfly who turned into a maggot – deconstruct.

Battle on, Son, and paint.

Turn back into that butterfly.

As I continued to read through my father's journey toward his death, I struggled to understand how someone could feel so low, be so down, desperate for help, beat themselves up so much, be in such a depressed state at such a young age. After all, he died when he was just 29, and this was three years prior to that. I started to see a confused man cry for help and enfold on paper with words of poetry, a message sent from his gifted hands, hands that were multitasking, one was letting his emotions flush out of him into his hands, down the pen, and onto the paper of his diary, and the other was wiping his cheek that was soiled with the emotional tears that flushed through his eyes. He was wounded, sorrowful, alone, feeling trapped in solitary confinement of his darkness, the cold frightening place many never dare to experience, the place with very little sunlight and dusty curtains, a place many wouldn't cope living in for a short stay.

This all came to me in a vision while reading the messages and projected feelings he wrote. From where I don't know; but the pain was felt, it took me back to that room with him when he was writing what I was reading. It was as real as the room I am in today, a strong image planted in my mind of a broken man and his surroundings.

I can't stop thinking about it, if only I was there to help him through his struggle, to release that tension and free his captive soul, isolated body, from the dark and lonely road that would lead to an end soon after that diversion. I know I could have brought him the light, and allowed him to see it, to feel its warmth and loving ray. I know because I have many gifts too, like my father. One is the ability to move others, influence them, connect, touch, inspire, and motivate them into a positive place, one they want to reach but are scared to take the first step, the step into the fear of not knowing what is on the other side.

I am not a psychologist, nor do I claim to be. I have never experienced this level of confusion, discomfort, never battled with my mental or emotional state like he has, but I still know

I could help because I have helped many people before, and because he is my father, my blood, I know I would not give up.

My strength comes from the physical struggles I have encountered, ones I welcomed, enjoyed overcoming and learning from, all of which I have had pleasure living through. In some disturbing way, I feel almost addicted to this way of living. I lean into it, look for opportunities, ones that will test me, all because I know what they will lead to and understand they are so important for my growth and development, for my adaption and evolution as a man and as a being. It is the same for the mind as it is for the body, it can be pushed to progress, I have witnessed it and lived through it. But it's easier to accept this when you are on the outside looking in. We often get blinded by the truth and the purpose to each given moment. Maybe my father recognized this pattern too. Perhaps he, like me, welcomed the pain, the struggles, leaned into them as I do, searched for opportunities to grow, but somewhere along his way, he got lost and it all became too much, too overwhelming, which left him in a turmoil, battling his demons, ones that would eventually lead him into the flames of the fire he died in.

Chapter 3
My Obsession

I often laugh to myself, sometimes out loud, about what I get great pleasure and satisfaction from. How I choose the toughest obstacles to overcome, most grueling events, looking for challenges and tests. Even the exercises to do in the gym, looking for new ways and ideas to stimulate not only my physical body but my sadistic mind, pushing through that pain but focusing on the pleasurable results it will give me, even in the moment when I feel ripped in half, as if my body is being operated on without the use of anesthetic, the feeling of waste products, the lactic acid torch deep in my muscle fibers, or when I have pushed my body to almost complete exhaustion, and like my lunges are tearing out of my chest, I'm struggling to breathe. My throat feels burnt, and my heart is beating so fast, too fast, it feels like it's going to explode. My core temperature is rising so high, my body become close to going into shock from overheating. I do this on a daily basis often while dieting so hard, almost starving myself to fit into a look I wish to present after hours of posing practice when I am more fatigued than I knew possible and question the fact, how am I still able to move? And, also, why am I still moving? Choosing to struggle for no reason beside the fact that I love to, which is a little weird, I know. It's hard to explain and understand unless you are wired like me, and I haven't met many people that are.

This is certainly not how life is meant to be. We are human beings. We like comfort and support, but this is life for me and one I am blessed to have woken up to.

Maybe it's my understanding of what such events will lead to, so instead of focusing on the painful now, I choose to focus on the future and only on the present when envisioning what the present will bring. That's another one of my gifts, teaching others to push through and what it will lead to, strength and power. Many will be surprised to know how much we can actually tolerate, block out, how our threshold increases, allowing us to withstand more and more, especially when we are only focused on the future, the pleasure the pain will lead to, the success that will come after it.

One good example is having a tattoo. We see many people sit in a chair for hours on end, having someone drag a cluster of fast-piecing needles down their flesh and injecting ink into it. They do this with ease, knowing it will be painful, but they are happy even in that moment, why? Because they are so focused on the beautiful artwork they will have displayed on the body for many people to see, for the meaningful portrait they have that represents a time in their life, a loved one's portrait reminding them of their connection, whatever it may be, but all because they will carry it with them, showcasing it proudly with pride, knowing they encountered some pain to have that pleasurable result on them for the rest of their life.

What you focus on in any given moment is so powerful, it can change your emotional state and your perception, and once you understand how the mind actually works, then it gets really exciting, like a game, a quest to be the best, to push our mind, body, and spirit to its limit and past, reaching new limitations and then realizing there is no limitation at all, only the ones we have created for ourselves.

Tattoo on my forearm

*

1987 In the art of creation the artist lives within

* John Kaler

This is one of the pains I was happy to bear, that would lead to a pleasurable result and a reminder of the truth. I have this poem written down my right forearm, along the ulnar bone, with my father's signature at the bottom, close to the hand, on my wrist.

I often get asked what it says, which I never get tired of explaining because it gives me another opportunity to tell others the meaning behind the words, and every time I do, I can tell a snippet of a story.

1987 is the year I was born, the year I was created by an artist which has now passed away but lives within me. His signature at the bottom is positioned just as it would if the artist was signing his work. It's positioned on my sleeve, so when I rest my arm on my chest, my hand on my heart, it lands right on it and I instantly have an ignited connection. His heart to mine, the source of all love, all energy, the second brain that moves the world in a positive direction. Through our instinct and intuition, our heart has the ability to save billions of lives, travel far distances to reach out to that person we love so deeply. Some would say you need to travel dimensions to reconnect with a spirit on the other side, but that depends on your personal beliefs. But what we do know is that it pulls like the strongest magnet we have ever felt with such a force, engagement, we find it hard to ignore until our souls connect, mesh, tangle together and become one.

I am aware that I have always looked at things from a different angle than most and see so much positive out of what others only see as negative. The darkest night is always met by the brightest morning, but the path to knowing is only a lonely one. I don't share this level of awareness, well not very often, so I choose to keep it inside, express it in another way by my poetry, my bodybuilding, my business, my passion in helping others. I think my father would have felt the same too, and another reason he didn't reach out and speak about his problems even when he was to the point of what seemed to be breaking. Maybe this is a lesson for me to talk more, share more, accept what others may think of me, spread my awareness, and not lock it in?

The diary

17 June '90

I feel like a fallen angel and that it would be easy to hate myself.

There is a small glimpse of hope and the hope stems from the people who still love.

Caroline, my mother, sister, and family. No one knows what I have experienced and what I am still experiencing.

I don't think the world has to and merely think that my personal world has to end, and good job too for my world has lost inspiration.

I know not what has really happened.

I just feel it's something bad or maybe something bad is about to happen. Controversy, I believe much good will happen for a lot of people.

There is hope, faith, although uncertainty is evident; the knowing of better is to come is something that very few people on this planet believe.

It somewhat feels surreal that I am here in the Philippines and I am surrounded by many joyful people, the kind my father speaks about meeting in his diary, spiritually enlightened beings connected with their souls, sharing love and happiness, sharing everything they have, giving without receiving. Many of them have less than most, but they are not connected to materialistic items, external belonging. They process something some of the richest ego-driven businessmen and women don't, peace and happiness within, the love for life themselves and all around them. My eyes are open, and so is my heart. I feel the love flow from around me, through me. This is overwhelming, the feeling of appreciation is something I envy, but I know it will change my perspective, shift my awareness onto what's important, who is important, and what this life is about, my purpose, and my deep desires I never knew were there.

This experience is already teaching me how to be more present in the now, to who I am, who I am with, and to what's around me, feeling all the gratitude, appreciation, acceptance, the wealth of being enriched with living a life in this incredible world.

As I read deeper into my father's diary, which is not easy at this point. I feel guilty for experiencing all this pleasure in my world, and at the same time he is experiencing all the pain in his. I feel as if this is all happening in the same time frame, like I am living the dream, while he is living the nightmare. Although I know I am reading the past whilst in the present, it is hard for me to escape this feeling of duality. He is so lost, struggling to deal with the painful present. I pray that he gets the help he needs before it's too late. I feel his refusal to the medication he was proposed and the therapy he was suggested to take, which is frustrating for me on the other side. My anger projects into conscious questions to why he isn't accepting this; why didn't he?

I felt him starting to lose faith, to give up, give in, as if his world was coming to an end, like he accepted his fate and the inevitable truth that his time was running out and his painful life was coming to a close, to the end of his book, his story, his journey to the other side.

I try to imagine how it must feel to take you to that point of realization, but it's very hard; it's not something I can comprehend. I don't think anyone can unless they too have been faced with these kinds of struggles. It's easy to criticize someone's reaction than it is to walk a mile in their shoes.

I am trying my best not to judge a man's situations, one that I have never been in or experienced something which is of comparison. But actually, come to think of it, I have been in many situations just like this, just in a different circumstance or environment. I am an athlete; I compete on an international level. I am a bodybuilder, and bodybuilding is a sport that requires so many sacrifices and an extreme-level discipline inside the gym and outside. Torturous workouts that seem never-ending as they take you closer to death and you only pray during that it will be better than what you are experiencing in that current moment. The diet restrictions are far from being an easy road. At times of eating so little food and burning so many calories, your insides feel like they are scraping away at the scraps left in the lining of your stomach and intestines as you move further into the waking day and that's just the start of it. It continues into the sleep or lack of, as you are often woken up throughout the night, brought away from the sleep you so desperately needed because your body is in pain and you feel like you are suffering. You get so annoyed because it took so long to switch your mind off to get into a slumber. It's like your brain in defense mode, feeling threatened for survival, so as soon as you knob off the hunger, pains get worst and you are brought straight back out into the chosen living reality. Feeling faint and dizzy is normal during daily tasks, and basic movements such as walking, even talking, and trying to string together a comprehensive conversation becomes a troubling task with a painful effort too, one you avoid even attempting. Thinking hurts, let alone talking, so you choose not to, which forces you to become isolated from the world in your own cocoon of pain, conserving as much energy as you can from avoiding doing the unnecessary, which at this point is a lot, you are so forced on winning you cut anything thing that has no benefit to the improvement of the way you look. This is all so you can forge enough energy to drag yourself to the gym, find the will to get under a loaded bar, rest it behind your neck, across your fragile traps, feeling the metal pressed deeply onto your skin-wrapped-shredded body. You restrict the weight from aggressively dragging you to the ground like you are falling from the sky but instead control the downward pull into a deep squat position, one that you cannot go any lower in if you wanted. You then find the power, the strength, the courage, and the confidence to roar your way back up until you are standing tall and proud again, defying all odds, then you continue this movement up and down until you are running on pure will, determination, and desire to not give up or not give in until finally you achieve what you have been seeking for, and that was to get to the point when you can no longer stand back up. To take your body to the point where it has nothing left, when you can no longer stand let alone stand up, where you actually fail, forced failure, and have no other option but to rerack the bar, drop to your knees, and collapse on floor from pure exhaustion. You lay there, heart beating, oblivious to what just happened, because the chances are you are blanked out, removed from all the background noise and are consumed only by the present moment, the task ahead. Thoughts start creeping back into the reservoir of collected data, you start to wonder how you were able to push your body that far, how miraculous it seems to find the strength to do that in these fatigued conditions, which give you an amazing feeling of self-awareness, of your strength, drive, capabilities, your endless possibilities of growth and progress. You feel so alive and happy knowing you did that; you made it through, a situation many would have quit or not even attempted. You gain such confidence and respect for yourself, but the job is not over. You feel the urge to get up and do it all again. You know if you can look up, you can get up, and if you can get up, you can do more, another exercise, another set, another spiritual experience that will take you one step closer, the opportunity to stare death in the face and have no fear, to take on the challenge knowing you are stronger than the thoughts of doubt and discomfort; you are you and you are unstoppable.

Just writing this now has not only got me psyched and pumped up but also got me reminiscing on past experiences: what I have been through, what I have overcome, the pain I met along my chosen path, the pain that led to so much pleasure. The difference being, I didn't see it as a barrier nor an obstacle, instead more like a stepping stone or a bridge to my future, a future where I am stronger, calmer, happier, and the best version of myself in all areas of my life that I can be. All this distracted me from what others normally experience, as I am driven on the end goal, the power of reason, the questions of why and the intuitive answers to all. I have been through many lows in my life for sure, been faced with tremendous struggle, challenges, setbacks, and sufferings of my own. I have been the witness and been victim of many tragic events and many unexpected loses in my family and in my close circle of friends.

Chapter 4
The Struggle Is Real

I lost my father when I was an infant and again when I was just a six-year-old boy, he was just 29. One year later, we were saying goodbye to my dad's mum who died of a broken heart after losing her son so suddenly. One year after she died, her husband, my dad's father, he left for the same condition as her. Maybe he thought it was time to leave, that life was not worth living, and that he was better with his wife and his son on the other side. Three deaths in two years, almost to the day, my father, my nan, my grandfather, all from the age of six years old to eight; I was still a young kid. That's pretty tough for anyone to deal with, especially in the early stages of life when your belief systems are being embedded, setting you up for life, how you will later look at such events, and how you will deal with them. The first eight years of your life are so important, they shape and mold your character, but your past doesn't define you, it doesn't control you, it doesn't stop you, it just teaches you lessons, ones that if you're smart enough you can learn from. I understand this now, but at that age, you don't know what to make of anything and you are not meant to. But when faced with such loss as a parent, it's hard to get over it because everywhere you turn, you meet questions which lead to your parents, who are they, what happened to your dad, your nan, granddad, which seem to carry the thoughts of these deaths on for longer than they should be, you try to avoid the conversation because its awkward for all conducting in conversation, not just you.

A few years later, before I was a teen, we had another tragic loss in the family, another one that would come with lots of questions and much confusion. We lost my uncle Wayne, my mother's brother, and we also lost my cousin Terry, my mother's sister's son. They both died on impact in a devastating car crash that left the car crushed and facing the opposite side around to the tree it impacted. It caused the destruction of the car and the deaths of three young people under the age of 30. There were two young ladies in the back too, but somehow, they both survived the accident.

From all these tragedies, the biggest was the loss of a family bond, the breakup and resentment this caused, which should have been the very reason the family got closer and stronger, but that was not in my power at that age to make right, or at least if it was, I wasn't yet aware.

The pain was tough at home, but going to school was another battle, with many rumors spreading around my school like wildfire. Nasty comments and more confusion which led to lots of irritation and distraction.

Kids would talk about how they were speeding, joyriding, and drink-driving. Some even said that they all deserved to die, which fueled violent eruptions in me, I was acting out aggressively as a young boy, using my fists as weapons or protective shields to the verbal assault I was attracting.

It wasn't a good time seeing my family get torn apart from one singular moment, circulated by helpless feelings of not yet being in position to change their views, witnessing my bulletproof mum suffer and live in grief, a mum that stood up against everything life threw at her. These are not pleasant memories from my life.

My good friend, Gavin Evans, left a print on me too when he left or when he was taken. We called him Scab. To this day I still don't know why, but it latched on and in a weird way suited him. We were friends for many years. Although he was a few years older, we grew up together. I was in school with his brother; we all hung out. We spent many nights out together, went on a vacation together as a group, but his life ended not long after. He got hit by car driven by an innocent elderly couple driving home one evening whilst traveling along the country lanes that were near the reservoir a few miles from Gavin's home. Gavin didn't have enough money to pay the taxi fare, the driver thought he was trying to pull a fast one and not pay the bill, so he thought it would be good to teach him a lesson, one that he would never forget, one that he would never remember. He drove him a few miles away from his home in the middle of nowhere, surrounded by darkness, a place many people don't pass, so Gavin could walk back and think about his actions and not behave like that again. Well, the taxi driver was certainly right. He wouldn't behave like that again, I think he had learnt his lesson on the walk to not his home but his grave, an early one that too before he was 30 years.

Lee's death was another shock to the system, especially after speaking to him a few hours before it was his time to go.

Lee was a good man, an honest, quiet guy that was built like a mountain but a gentle giant. He was a good friend and he helped me massively over the years when I first found the love and passion for lifting weights. He was like a mentor of mine but never would claim that title. He was one of the only guys I knew that were bodybuilders, he and another good friend of mine, Michael Kitto, who was very close friends with Lee. They took me under their wing, teaching me the fundamentals, the basics, guided by their experience and steered away from the mistakes they made. They passed on their wealth of knowledge to me and I couldn't be more grateful at the time and even to this day. At the gym, the day I last saw him, we chatted about his plans of competing that coming year, as the bodybuilding season was underway and that's usually all we spoke about. Lee said he was off home to spend some quality time with his beautiful wife that he admired and to play with his newborn baby girl. That was the real trophy in his life and what brought the most success his human body could bring.

The next morning, I received a call from another close friend with the sad news that Lee was dead. His wife, Sarah, had found him on the bathroom floor that morning where he had been lying for many hours.

He had woken up to go to the toilet in the middle of the night and had a heart attack whilst everyone was asleep in silence.

It wasn't a nice experience carrying the coffin of a good friend down the cemetery to hoist him into the ground where he would be buried, past his beautiful wife and his cute sweet daughter as the tears ran down their faces and the desperate hope that maybe all that is, is not true.

I think the most upsetting of all loses was a few years ago back in 2017, shortly before my wife and I made the move to Dubai; the event would change many lives forever.

It was around 10 at night. I returned home from a training session with my coach and we spent some time after checking my progress, my condition, and discussing any tweaks that needed to be in place for a competition I was preparing for, I was seven weeks out from Mr. Wales. I left in the morning after my cardio. I was back-to-back with personal training clients all day, then I would make the trip to see him at his gym, train, pose, and come home to shower, eat, and start it all again. It was a long and exhausting day; it always is at that point on prep. I walked in, took my shoes off, and went straight upstairs to see my wife as she was in the bedroom, drying her hair in her pjs.

She just got off the phone with her auntie and she looked a little concerned.

"My mum has fallen down."

I asked if her mum was okay. She said, "I think so, she is in the hospital, but my auntie said not to worry, she is fine."

She didn't seem convinced to be honest; it was a confused tone.

"Do you want to go up to see if she is okay?" I gestured in a soft and supportive manner.

She was very hesitant in her reply, "No…it's late…you just got home and you are on prep; you have had a long day."

I firmly said, "If you feel like you should go and want to go, then let's go…I want to go too."

We jumped straight in the car and arrived at the hospital by 10:15 p.m. We joined her mum's sister Liz, who Carly lived with for many years before she moved in with me. There were others present there too, her mum's partner Steven, her uncle Dai, brother Owen, and cousin Jamie. They were all sitting in the waiting room and so we joined them as well until the doctor came out and said that two of us could go in and visit Sarah. Carly and her auntie went in to see her mum and the rest of us waited patiently, not thinking much of it, laughing and joking, not really taking the matter too seriously. It was something we were quite used to with Sarah. We had been there before; she had fallen a few times, mostly after she had a few too many drinks, which was more often than not, bless her.

After around 30 minutes or so, they both came out. My wife was crying her heart out. I ran over to see what the matter was because this was a shock to me. I don't think either of us was prepared for what she witnessed. Her auntie kept saying, "See, this is why I didn't want to tell you. I didn't want you to see your mum like this." She was crying too.

I was still in confusion. "What's wrong, babe?" I asked.

"My mum, my mum…she is all wired up… There're all pipes coming out of her," she blurted out with a cry.

I've never seen my wife this upset; she was hurting. It hurt me too, not only because my mother-in-law was in that way but I felt my wife's pain inside me. We are connected, soul mates, we are one. I hugged her and told her that everything would be okay, that I was there for her.

After two long days and longer nights of preparing for the unexpected, we held onto a glimmer of hope. Two days of doctors giving us the upsetting breakdown of Sarah's situation and condition, which was tough to take in let alone digest and absorb. Every second of every minute of every hour of the day seemed to trickle more emotions into a flooding pool that was very close to over-spilling and washing down the faces.

We were told that even if she pulled through the coma she was in and had been for several days, the quality of life would be massively affected and that she would have suffered from severe brain damage. They advised us to take her off all the life-support machines that were keeping her alive, give her a chance to bring herself up until her last breath, and in the process, we would hope and pray for a miracle.

Sarah Louise Smith died at the age of 47, two days after going into hospital for the last time but this time with all her loved ones, friends, and family around her. During the last few hours of being alive, after laying in the hospital unconsciously, she miraculously came back into awareness and found enough strength to come back around for a few short minutes. She held her sons' hands and my wife's, then told them how proud she was of them and how sorry she was to put them through all she did. She was consciously aware of us all and she was making her peace before finally disconnecting her beautiful soul from the body she was birthed into and gave birth from.

The most tragic thing about her death was how it happened. She had fallen over one night, drunk, she hit her head on the floor, which caused her to have a fit. The fit caused her to go into shock and she vomited, she then lay there unconsciously for several hours before being found by her son. Doctors said that vomit made its way into her lungs, which brought on pneumonia and as she was laying there for some time, there was very little hope for her, especially with her health not being in the best shapes.

That was also a coffin that was tough to carry, not because of the weight but because of the person's body that was nested inside it.

The weeks that followed were tough for us, but despite the pain, I continued my preparation for the next seven weeks toward the contest, didn't miss a meal or a workout, and went on to win Mr. Wales.

There are many memories like this, events that would normally sway many people's direction or at least distract them from staying focused on their goals. I know because I work with these people every day. They are some of my clients. But nothing ever seems to stop me from moving forward and staying disciplined, driven, and willing to push through anything and not give up, staying positive in every situation, and encouraging those around me to do the same, helping other become a better person, the best version of themselves inside and out by having faith and desire.

Rewinding back to when I was ten years old, I had a pet dog named Floss. He was so cute, so loyal, he followed me everywhere; he was my best friend.

One day, I went home to get Floss and take him with me out for playing. My mum wasn't home. She was down her friend's, so the front door was locked, but being summertime, Floss was out in the garden where he had shade, water, and the freedom to run and entertain himself for a short while. I jumped over the gate and opened it up, and he followed me out.

In that moment, I remember hearing a little voice in my head say to me, "You know your mum told you never to take Floss out without a lead." I spoke out loud with my reply, "He will be fine... He stays close to me." I ran up to my friend Kyle Evans's, younger brother to Gavin Evans, the one that got hit by the elderly couple and died, grandfather's house. I ran as fast as I could, like an energetic, eager, young boy that did not want to miss out on anything, Floss was running beside me of course!

Kyle's grandfather lived in a big bungalow, the biggest in the area. It featured a massive garden with wooden swings, ponds, big trees, loads of fun stuff to get dirty playing with; a perfect place for imaginations to run wild. Leading up to the bungalow was a long driveway which came directly on to the Heads of the Valley, which was the main road leading to either ends of the country, ideal for the businessman he was.

Whilst we were playing on the swings, Kyle's grandfather's dog ran out, straight to Floss, and chased him down the long driveway leading toward a fast-flowing main road. "Floss, Floss!" I shouted and then screamed so hard, it felt like my throat was ripping, desperately trying to stop him from running down to the road. Eventually, he did stop. He stopped dead, dead into a white van traveling faster than the 70/mph speed limited, and that was the reason the driver didn't stop.

I ran down the driveway in the hope that he would somehow be alive, but there was no chance. My best friend lay on the ground with no life left in him, so I just kept running, running past him in shock of seeing him lay so breathless. I kept running and didn't stop until I reached the house, I knew my mum was in. I banged on the door. Somehow, she knew it was me. I gasped for air and blurted out, "Floss is dead, Mum, he is dead," as I dropped to my knee and the realization of what just happened sunk on my desperate soul.

By the time I reached home a few minutes later, my friends brought Floss down from the accident and placed him in my garden. I just grabbed a shovel, dug a big hole, put him in, and started covering him with the fresh soil I just dug out. I padded it over with the shovel firmly, then walked over to the pavement, grabbed a chalky stone, and, in big letters, I wrote the word 'FLOSS.' With the tears running down my face and as I cried my heart out, I put him to rest in the ground and put the emotions I felt to rest too. The next day and the days after, I didn't even mention his name or talk about the innocent being; I buried him, buried it and moved on.

Looking back, writing down a few of the experiences I have lived through and bringing them to context allows me to see how my character was built, and with the mindset and understanding I have now, I know that it could be for what is to come: bigger challenges, struggles I may face, more pain that I have never experienced, more than I have ever imagined.

So many documented, imprinted memories of mine I have witnessed first-hand has taught me what I am able to tolerate, what I can take and keep moving. It is as though I was born to receive them, deal with them, learn from them, and show others that it's not over, that with a positive attitude and faith in knowing everything will be better and that good is to come, we can make it through whatever life throws at us, and, believe me, life throws a hell of a lot.

All these thoughts and memories allowed me to open up a doorway in my mind to areas I hadn't explored yet but knew they were always there. I found a seed planted in my mind, but only when I open the door that's containing it and let the light in is when it starts to grow, flourish, and I start to revisit a very impacting day of my past life.

The day was May the 9th, 1993, 26 years ago. I am a six-year-old, blonde-haired, chubby, cute-faced, young pup. I am wearing a coded waist jacket, white shirt, black tie, black trousers, and smart, polished shoes. My hair is combed smartly to the side, all but the right side. That's where my cowlick stands proudly. I am holding my mother hand tightly; she is holding mine tighter. We are walking out of the church where my father's coffin laid to rest after the ceremony.

My mum looks at me. She tries to smile, but her cheeks barely move. They are lifeless. I notice the red, teary eyes, the running mascara down her soft, pink cheeks. She wants to look away from the uncomfortableness, but our eyes are locked together, but eventually she looks ahead after a struggle to disconnect. We continue to walk through the crowd of people that respectfully came to give their blessing and watch us walk out of the church. There are so many familiar faces, it feels as if everyone that's here I know and that they know me too, although I am used to seeing them, but not like this, with a completely different impression on their faces, the same one my mum has on hers. They are all sad, upset, but it feels like it's more for me than them. I can feel the sympathy that flows from their tilted heads surround me; there are so many too, it's hard to ignore because they are all looking at me.

So much sadness in this cold, silent air that it overflows like rivers after a lashing from Mother Nature with downfall. In this very moment, it is apparent to me that my dad was and is still very important; he is well-known. He will be missed by many, and they all came for him, to see him off to the other side.

I feel the pressure from everyone. I feel overwhelmed, cornered into a confined space, but yet I continue walking down the path that seems to be never-ending. To where it leads, I don't know. I feel like I am in a bad dream, one I wish to wake from. I'm confused. I can't understand why everyone's so upset and crying. I start to question myself.

Why am I not crying?

Should I be?

Maybe that's why they won't stop looking at me. Maybe they will only stop if I start?

I wanted them to stop; it's too intense. I am fighting a battle I can't win because I am outnumbered.

I bleed out a tear from my dry ducts, one that I had to force to start, but the rest seem to flow off more easily. I'm crying my little heart out. I joined in with the crowd. I feel normal, together, no longer alone. I drenched my face with a sad look on it, but my heart remained fresh. I feel no pain, no sorrow. I am not at all upset. I feel nothing, but my appearance is expressing a feeling I haven't experienced. I was simply modeling those that stare at me. This seems to bring more sadness to them; they cry more. But I wasn't emotional about this day or the passing of my father. I am only crying because in this moment I feel it is the right thing to do.

The reason I am not upset in any way is not because I don't love my father or that I don't want to see him again. I don't feel upset, sad, or like I want to cry because in this moment I realized something. I realize that my father hasn't left, he is still here with me. I feel him just as strong as I did yesterday and last month, last year. He loves me and I feel his spirit.

The diary

Dear creator

Thank you for those brief moments of joy

I wish I had more respect for life

I respect the lives of others

I hate pain and suffering and to watch it is the worst fear of all.

I trust you will look after all.

Please protect everybody

I can't believe what I see on T.V.

Where are the angels now?

I don't want this responsibility, but it seems I have it or had it.

I'm no mistake but am prepared to take full responsibility to some rest.

I am afraid and ready to be judged. I take full blame. I am guilty. But I believe in you and in your love. I am not that well-educated.

Please let the people of Gwent help me. I cannot bare to see more chaos.

I am not much good now it seems

I don't know what the answer is

I dint listen to you I am sorry.

I am not sure the chaos it be illusion.

All I wanted was everyone to find happiness, but I could not find it myself.

I do understand right from wrong, but I still have done wrong. I'm a week person, still I am confused.

They say it's a case of us and them.

Does this mean good and bad

There is both in everyone.

Some people are very good, some are not so. Me, I'm confused.

I love people, I hate violence, yet I have had violent thoughts.

I enjoy the company of good friends.

I want to work and live, but now things seem haywire. I wake and birds don't sing like they used to. Mike Bradhan is a great teacher; I wish he could help me.

Sad I am,
a poor pathetic man,
so alone,
here on my own.
I've been so confused with the voices outside my head.
Sometimes I can't tell whether I'm alive or dead.
But a man can't be happy all the time, it's true.
There is a cup of sorrows which make a man blue.

Chapter 5
My Intuition

During the short flight from Cebu in the Philippines to Singapore, I read the last page of my father's diary. My trip to the Philippines created a spark in my heart and so did my father's diary. But before I made my way back to Dubai to put all the pieces to the puzzle together and to explore new ventures in life, it was time to explore the city I had heard so much about as I made a short stop off. I knew by the time the day was over I would feel fully charged, recharged, focused, motivated, inspired, determined, and alive, all of the positive things you could hope to be. I knew the rest of the year was going to be amazing; the future was bright; I was being led to an incredible life.

My father's diary was quite an emotional read to say the least. In fact, it was very tough. I was battling with the emotions he was releasing, absorbing his thoughts and pain.

The closer I got to the last few pages, the closer to the end of his life, as that is what the diary led too, the more my father was crying for help. He seemed to have understood what was wrong with him. Well, at least he thought he did. He kept telling me that the Devil was after him, that there was no escape, no end, no way out from his manipulation. He came to the realization that it was not his mind that was causing all the problems he was facing, it was an evil source, one that he had opened up to, one that was hunting him down, haunting him, isolating him from the rest, cornering him, chasing him in the direction of the grave he lay in.

It's like a disturbing horror story of entrapment, a story that I was always meant to read, a story I was meant to tell.

These thoughts were going through my mind just after I read the last word, and that's when I felt inspired, when I felt moved to do something big. My intuition was stronger, my mind was opened and exposed to an incredible rollercoaster of a man's life, a life that was short-lived, but the story brought back a side that many didn't see. I was able to see that many other people are also experiencing a similar pain, a destructive story for themselves as they turn each painful page, but instead of reading it, they are living it.

Why was the diary written and kept, was it for me?

What is the message?

You have to tell it!

You have to write a book and share this message!

I spoke out loud and listened to my own voice, but the words fell from somewhere else, a cosmic space, not within physical touch but available to receive thoughts from another and tap into to share thoughts of your own.

I got excited and thought now is the perfect time as I sat in my chair, all fired up with excitement, motivation, and drive.

I have the coaches and the right connections that can help me publish this book, I thought, *and maybe one day you can make it into a movie.* I could play my dad, after all, I look and act like him. All these thoughts and ideas sparked my imagination and questions like, how would I start the movie, where would it be filmed, and who would be in it, came to my mind. I grabbed my mobile, looked up the name Jake

Director, and I was about to message him with this idea and arrange a meeting when I heard another voice, but this time in my head and not out loud, *Slow down, boy, let's stay calm, you have plenty of time, you have so much going now, so relax, buddy, it's coming!*

I sat back in my chair, took a deep breath in, closed my eyes, and smiled. I held my breath in before slowly letting all the air empty my lungs whilst filling my mind with gratitude, love, and appreciation for being alive and inspired to inspire.

Jake, the director, was a guy I got introduced to by a good friend. Suzie is a very successful woman. She modeled for years, has been in many commercials and ads, and is now an aspiring actor. Jake was the director in a movie Suzie was playing a lead part in, an independent movie which had an international cast. Jake was looking for someone to play a bodyguard for Suzie's daughter in the movie, and I seemed to fit the role. Suzie arranged a meeting with him at her house. He liked me, and he said, "Shave the beard into a goatee and you're in." He gave me the script with the highlighted scenes I would be in. Three days later, we were setting off to stay on Sir Baniyas Island for four days, on set for most of them, starting very early and finishing very late, where we would film a large chuck of the movie. There were many other scenes to shoot but all of which we could do from Dubai.

What may seem bizarre about this connection is not what it led to or what it can potentially lead to in the future but how we actually got connected in the first place.

Like I mentioned, Suzie was a good friend. I would see her often at the gym I worked in, but I hadn't seen her for a while, but one afternoon whilst I was driving to the gym, I remember thinking, I wonder if Suzie could get me a part in a movie, because it is something I really want to do and I know she is pushing her career, but at this time I had no idea who Jake was or that she was about to play a main role in his movie.

Thirty minutes later, I get a call from Suzie. "Hi, Christian. I am sitting down with the director and producer of a movie I am playing a lead role in and he is looking for someone to play a bodyguard for my daughter. I thought of you because you're big, strong-looking, and I know you are committed. Would you like to come and meet him on Tuesday at mine?" It was a few days later, I said yes. I went to her home to meet him and there it was. I was on the big screen at the cinema, playing a bodyguard to one of the main leads.

Many would think that this is a coincidence, in fact that's how I used to think actually. But these conscious outputs, my intentions leading to my reality happen all too often to label them as the above.

It's mostly with things I want. When I think about it, it seems to show up, somehow, somewhere, like my thoughts are being listened to by the universe. But what I realize is that it is never served on a silver plate ready to feast, it is presented as an opportunity accompanied by a tough decision, delivered at the crossroads, that is surrounded by a wall of fear!

Another example of my vibrant ability was when I was in Bohol on the event with my coach, J.T. Foxx. J.T. is a very intimidating guy, and although I am very confident, loud, powerful, and strong, I get so nervous when speaking in front of a group. Meetings where I have to introduce myself is something I avoided for years, even turned down opportunities because of my fear to speak publicly. I believe it stems back to when I was in school and I used to get worried when reading out loud to a classroom of pupils, getting nervous that I would not be able to read the sentence correctly. Maybe I got laughed at one time, I don't remember, but what I do remember is pretending I needed to go to the toilet when it was almost my turn to stand up and read.

Weeks leading up to the top one-percent event, I would get daunted by the thought of standing up in front of the other entrepreneurs talking about my business. I asked the organizers several times if I was being coached in a group or together because of my concern, not to avoid but to be prepared. It was literally making me lose sleep.

Although one of my goals was to get over this fear and learn public-speaking skills to help me stand up and talk, to sell, sell my beliefs that we can achieve anything we desire if we work hard and believe we can do it. Also, I was aware that the bigger the platform, the bigger the audience, and the more people I could positively impact and deliver my messages to, but I was held back, I was holding myself back.

Whilst in Bohol, I remember thinking, I really want to speak onstage, but I need to get over my fear first. Then one evening, I felt it, that strong feeling you can't ignore. I knew it was coming. I rang my wife and told her that, "Tomorrow something big is going to happen. I can feel it, but I don't want to tell you what it is, but remember me saying it, and when it happens, I will tell you what it was I knew was going to happen."

The following day, the last day of that event, I was sitting down with J.T., running by an idea we had come up with and that's when it happened, exactly like I knew it would, like a play I had already watched in my mind the day before. We were sitting down. He was facing me with his legs crossed and he said, "I want to put you on stage, speaking for me in three weeks' time in front of a thousand people." He suggested I talk about my background, my business, the results I have had so far working with a coach, and to deliver a message to them that would inspire and motivate them. Without overthinking too hard about my reply to him, without letting my fear build up, or the voices in my head of self-doubt, becoming face to face with my biggest fear, but this time it was on steroids, I quickly said, yes, I'll do it!

This was the big thing I knew was going to happen that day from the day before.

I had three weeks to prepare a speech, get over my nerves and anxiety, face my fears, but with my belief and faith as well as understanding the power of my thoughts, seeing what was to come before it did, I was confident because I also knew I would get up on that stage, they would love my speech, and I would love the experience and it would lead to many more. So, I did, they did, and it did lead to more!

During the flight to Dubai, I found myself in and out of thought and feeling, passing over oceans of ripples that send out more waves to the shores they crash on.

Viewed from above the clouds of happiness and peace, but yet there is tension in the air.

It is felt and not seen or heard, but I know it's there, and soon it will become more apparent than ever.

I have a strong gut feeling. I have always had a strong intuition, but now it's more vibrant than before, too much to ignore or pass over.

It's like I am more inline, aligned, more connected with the source.

Poetry flows to me, like I'm bathing in a river of awareness. Is it because I finally finished reading my father's diary, one where he expressed his confused, depressed state, painful experience, and emotional state, one that led him into the grave? It seemed like he wanted to go after losing sight of hope, faith, and appreciation.

I know that I was going back to a place where I seemed to have forgotten that I did not enjoy being in.

They say there is no place like home, which I agree, but home is not always as comforting as it could be, especially when you are sharing it with others, especially if those others don't share the same space as you and somewhat distraught your reality, or maybe it is you that is actually doing the energy bending, as I am aware, we can warped all around us to fit into whatever we desire and often enough we are not even aware.

There was tension between my wife and I, it had been from some time. We tried to ignore it but we never could and the question, why try to ignore? Is being ignorant to truth ever going to lead to a positive outcome?

Maybe, I am not, but it didn't work for us. Perhaps it is better that confronting the situation and dealing with drama, yes, better but less productive in regaining peace with no drama.

My wife was on her own path and we were not getting on like we used too, we were friends still, and loved each other but there wasn't the support we once both offered.

The fact that she turned down the opportunity to come on this trip with me, to learn more about business, and tick of another country to explore was not sitting well with her, but furthermore, the fact that I was here with a friend was too much, which she had expressed whilst I was on this trip.

I was finding myself, meeting people, experiencing the world, getting excited about the future and planning the path towards it. And she was at home, getting on with her days, which I know she wished she had come not only to support but to experience too.

The way I saw it, I asked her to come, wanted her to come, but she clearly didn't want because of work commitments, she said, and that she didn't want to use her holidays to come away with me and wanted to keep them for, 'the holiday of the year,' her birthday, as I always take her somewhere special. But we both know she could have come if she wanted too.

I was going anyway, I didn't see it any other way and the fact I had someone else to go with, someone I trusted, that encouraged me, was something I was extremely grateful for. I knew I would have more confidence to stand up and speak, to get over my fear and to relax my guard so I could let more in.

But it did get me thinking about the situation from another perceptive whilst I was away, especially since a few people had reached out to me too, including another one of my mentors, my bodybuilding coach. He said that I should be careful. I will end up single if I act like this with no consideration for my wife's feeling, the ones I may not be aware of until it was too late.

I always was happy to get away to be honest, and not have to worry about other people's feeling, I was tired with that, I needed to get away from the negative energy I felt at home, and focus on me, what I need, want I want. As selfish as it seems, I believe almost every act of kindness is, as we are always seeking what makes us happy, even if that is listening, and help other people, as the feeling it gives them, which then give us, is why we have motive to do it.

Not to mention the fact this trip cost me around 7,500 pounds, it was an investment, and there was no way I was missing this, it was the beginning of something huge, I could feel it, and I grabbed it.

This was a very important trip to me, one I needed and knew would lead to so much more if I was in a calm and collective state of mind, free from all the noise and pollution.

Another reason I know my wife was upset from the day I booked the trip was because I didn't ask her before I signed up for the coaching, and it was an investment that I believe she felt she should have input in.

The truth is, when I want to do something, and I feel a strong pull, it feels like I am being guided from another, and I trust the source and don't want to sway my decision and be persuaded from taking it, so I tend not to ask advice, I just do it. But maybe this is a lesson, maybe it all is, there seems to be a lot of opportunities to learn from, one's I was once blinded too, but am now seeing a little more clearly.

It was tough being away from Carly; we never spent this much time apart like we had now, 11 days. That is the longest to date, even when we didn't live together and she was visiting on the weekends until she moved in six months later.

I am so excited to get back to my wife, my life, my structure, I missed her and missed it all. I landed back in Dubai around 1 p.m. and would be straight back at it. I had my first client at 3 p.m., just two hours. It took 30 minutes to get home.

The plan was to spend a little time with her, have a meal together, catch up on the last 11 days, show her my business plans, shower, then head back out the door to the gym where I would be back-to-back until late that night. It's the life of an entrepreneur, a hustler, always moving, pushing, grafting, and doing what I can to get to the next step which is always a big leap away.

I got home to our apartment, but the door was locked. She never left the key at reception like she said she would, which was odd, and to top it off, my battery went on the flight. Great, I had all my luggage with me, had no food; I didn't eat on the plane because I am a bodybuilder and only eat plain, simple food, which I am a little obsessed about too. I needed a shower because I felt rough and wanted to make a good impression for my clients that afternoon. I was thinking, *this can't be a good sign*. She knew I was home at this time. Is it really going to be this way?

I jumped in another taxi, this time to a place of Carly's work which luckily wasn't far from where we live. I knocked on the blacked outdoor of the salon Carly manages, which is a women-only hair-and-beauty salon.

She opened the door like as if she knew it was me. She said hi in her usual, high-pitched, extended tone which sounds like a melody, but her face was a little off. I went to give her a kiss as I told her I missed her, but she turned away from me and said, "It's Ramadan!" Ramadan is the holy month, and in the Middle East, many things are prohibited, like showing affection in public, drinking, or eating before certain hours, music in public areas. Many businesses close for the hours of fasting too, which is from sunrise to sunset, even restaurants, coffee shops, etc. So that's understandable, even for respect in a Muslim country, but that wasn't why she turned away from me. I could tell she wasn't happy and aware she was also making me aware, so I accepted it, took it and the key off her, jumped back in the taxi, got back home, quickly cooked my food, showered, got changed, had a coffee, and went on my way to transform lives and give my clients the energy they missed for the last few weeks whilst trying not to think about the fact that after a long day, I would be returning back to the same environment I did before I had left.

The feeling was back, home now had that feeling I forgot, and I hadn't even been back for long at all.

The butting heads, disagreeing with everything, not seeing eye to eye anymore, and often spending more time apart than together even when in the same room.

The diary

I feel like the fallen angel and it would be easy to hate myself.

There is a small glimmer of hope and the hope stems from the people that still love me.

No one knows what I've experienced and still experiencing.

I don't think the world has to and I merely think that my personal world has to, and good job too for my personal world has lost inspiration.

I know not what has happened. I just feel something bad or maybe something bad is about to happen.

Controversy, I believe that much good will happen for a lot of people.

Chapter 6
My Queen

Beauty and the beast, that's what some say, but every thug needs a lady.

My queen, my soul mate, my everything, my life, my wife.

Carly Louise Williams, such a powerful being that gives off vibrant power that is felt even when unintended. She stands just over five ft. tall, slim, toned, and has curves in all the right places. Her golden wavy hair frames her beautiful face that projects her ocean-like eyes which seem to pull you in with an urge to explore the depths beyond them. Her plumb and sweet lips showcase the caring smile she wears and an expression that glares positive energy that carries her spirit forward.

Many say that I am lucky to have her in my life, which I agree, but I am more of a believer in fate, and faith, than luck if I am honest, we were meant to be, the story of two that become one, that was us.

She is an incredible person, that's for certain. She is an inspiration to me. So, loving, she loves me so much, loves everyone, and everyone loves her. She is extremely trustworthy, she is a big part of my support network too, which is small but tight. She is my guider; I trust her opinion over many others. I ask for it with my decisions, my goals, ideas, career, relationships, my business, even when it comes to bodybuilding. This is an area I ask very few their opinion on, with regards to my progress or lack of, especially on prep, because I want honest feedback on how I am looking. Carly will always tell me straight, to the point, no beating around the bush or sugarcoating her words. Even on the day of a competition I have prepared for months in advance, even years, if I am not looking my best, she will let me know, to let me see what I look like from the outside, something I may be blinded to in that fragile, fatigued mindset.

I will admit, her deliverance on such topics is not always welcomed, nor is it appreciated on times, but her honesty is, so I admire that she will never tell me what I want to hear but always what I need to.

Carly is such a kind, loving person, with a unique soul, one that I was drawn to and couldn't let go. There is a reason why we have been together for ten amazing years. We have traveled to many incredible places in the world. We have a library of stories from the adventures we've been on. In ten years, we have lived in nine different homes, which doesn't even make sense to me or add up, because it seemed we have had years of memories in each one.

As a couple, we have always been spontaneous; we just went with the flow and got up and did it. Our wedding was no exception, we only planned it four days before we said our vows at the top of the tallest building in Las Vegas, the Stratosphere, at 6 p.m. on November 2nd, 2014. We overlooked the most breathtaking view of the sunset that shone its last rays of light above the towers that make up panoramic view of a city that never sleeps.

We even jumped out of a plane 14,000 feet in the sky together. Well, she got dragged and thrown out, literally, but that story can wait for another time.

Falling in love sometimes happens in a single moment, love at first sight, when you know they are the one; I knew she was. I felt it deep inside, right in my core, like my heart had connected to another instantly and at the same time I realized how there was a gap in my heart that I wasn't aware of until that gap was filled with the missing half.

Our relationship was as if the story was already lived before and we were just telling it day by day, week by week, year by year, since the day we both united, or reunited, it depends on your beliefs.

Carly and I dated for six months before she moved into my first home away from the family, the one she helped me pick several weeks before. It was like a little penthouse pad that I rented 25 miles from where we both lived in Merthyr Tydfil, the valleys. I decided to move to Cardiff, the capital of Wales, where I would build a career and become recognized in the fitness industry.

Since Carly moved in with me, we have been together almost every day since. We traveled a lot but mostly with each other. We had big plans to move to America, Australia, Canada, somewhere bigger and better than where we were living. After visiting Dubai, we both fell in love again but with a place this time, as we were already in love with each other.

Carly was offered a job working in a salon, the one she now manages, so we made the move in October 2017. I started my own fitness company, one where I could employ personal trainers, a marketing team, sales team, whoever I needed to help grow the company and expand the brand.

I was in my element, training many clients at some of the best gyms in the world, connecting with like-minded people and developing my career further, pushing myself but in return developing so much.

Carly was not enjoying Dubai as much as I was, her experience wasn't delightful or at least she didn't show the same enthusiasm as I did. She seemed unhappy, struggling to settle into the Dubai lifestyle. The workload was too much for her, I guess, as it is a lot different than the U.K. Six days a week, every week, long hours, plus she didn't drive and the commute to and from work was adding another two hours on top of a 12-hour shift.

But I saw it as a steppingstone, one that would help her gain more experience and her foot in the door to climb. I tried my best to make her feel more positive about the place. I wanted to make her feel better, but I also really didn't want to move back to the U.K. I wanted to stay; I loved it, loved what I did, this suits me just fine. The long hours, I'll take them. I am used to the grind and grafting my way to success, chasing my goals, looking for new challenges, seeking the uncomfortable, the unstable, even the uncertain, because that's what drives me.

Carly on the other hand prefers more of a work-life balance, more family time, home time, down time. She has certainly calmed me down a little over the years, as I was even more relentless and obsessive before, but still, it is not something I can easily switch off. It's weird in me, like I was born for it.

After we were living in Dubai for around 12 months, which is not very long ago, our relationship started drifting slightly and then faster more recently. Our energies were not aligned, our opinions were debated, our thoughts seemed far from what they were, or at least that is how it felt. The frequency we were vibrating at was changing, so were our views, and our routines too.

Things were so different from when we were back in Wales. It was rare for us to be sitting and eating together now, waking up together or going to bed at the same time together, we were coming and going, communicating on passing, which is nothing like it was before.

We were spending less time together, and when we did spend time, it wasn't of quality. It was like we weren't interested in each other as much as were and we weren't afraid to show it.

We would go for dinner and be on our phones, when at home we'd be on laptops. We may have been in each other's company, we may have been together, but we were not really, our attention and focus were elsewhere.

Our groups of friends changed, and we found different ways to socialize that didn't match each other's idea of fun.

I would catch up with friends at the gym or a coffee shop. Carly would go out drinking and socializing with many of her new friends, which was something she never really did.

There were many occasions when she would go out randomly after popping to the mall, not tell me, then come home early morning when I was getting up for my cardio as the sun was rising.

We were becoming distant, our conversations were either stale, pointless or frustrating, like we were butting heads with each other over the silliest things. We were snapping for no reason, irritated and annoyed with what each other was doing or wasn't doing.

I was confused and often questioned if was I to blame. Was it all me?

Was I that hard to live with and be married to?

I remember thinking to myself, maybe it's because I am a bodybuilder which takes a lot of focus and sacrifice. Perhaps she has had enough of this restricted lifestyle, not going out drinking with her or eating out when I am in preparation mode. But then, even after the competition was over, things were the same. I again took the blame, well, blamed myself. Maybe it's because I'm so driven on my future and career, that I am working till late, working every weekend. Maybe it's because I am always looking for more work to fill my time. Perhaps she has had enough of my boring lifestyle and is craving more attention.

These are some of the thoughts I would constantly think over as I lay in bed at night and she lay beside me with an empty distance between us which was once filled with vigorous passion.

Maybe it was just the time we're in, I thought, where we are in our lives, careers, where we want to go.

Perhaps our currency had changed. What we value in a partner and what we expect to receive in exchange for our love. Maybe it's us that has changed, separately but together; we were no longer a match.

What made the conversation about how we have changed more difficult to open and discuss was the fact that she had not long ago lost her mum, and I thought maybe that was the reason she was acting differently toward me. Maybe that's why she wasn't as positive as she was before, before the shock that left painful wound, one that was still fresh.

Carly was never one to express herself and share her feeling or emotions. She pushed them down deep, aside, away from the surface, where they could hide, and stay buried.

It was clear to see, because I saw that when I first met her, and it is one of the things that drew me in, I knew under that shield of armor, there was an innocent gem, and I accepted her for who she was and who she presented.

So, I never asked her or discussed the matter much to be honest. I instead made sure she knew I was there for anything she needed from me, well at least I thought I did.

Whatever was the reason why we were becoming more separated, we both could not deny the truth. It was something we both could feel growing stronger but also growing us apart. Not many people around us knew what we were going through, we seemed to mask it quite well, like acting in our own movie, playing a role, pretending to everyone, including ourselves, ignoring the signs, blind to the potential truth that we may have to face, or turning a blind eye, waiting for the eyes to finally meet, and we all know the eyes never lie, they are the gateway to one's soul, and the soul is truth.

Not all marriages last forever, everyone that gets married thinks they will live happily ever after, but it's not always the case.

Marriage is a working process, sometimes you can deviate off the line you were once bound to, the connection that ignited the excitement that carried you through many incredible experiences together can become to harder to hold, the candle flame may start to dim, and the spark is harder to light.

Many people have confessed to me in banter, but I sensed the truth behind the laughter when they said that if it wasn't for their children, they would have had a divorce; their marriage ended many years ago.

But I strongly believe that when you meet the one person you are meant to spend the rest of your life with, it doesn't dim or die. You always bring the best out of each other, accommodate each other, have unconditional love for each other, and have so much love that you each become unstoppable.

You are connected from above by spiritual codes that are so deep, they go back further than your life's existence.

You are perfectly engaged, born into this life for the purpose of each other, to find your soul mate, reconnected in this form, and cause a massive explosion of light, love, and energy, like a supernova that powers a life of incredible experience, and memories. The collision of beings ignites the world for everyone to see and witness the beautiful love bond that is unbreakable.

I am writing this from my own personal experience because that was exactly what Carly and I had little over 12 months ago, which was incredible, like a magical fairytale. But now it's fading fast, which leaves me wondering in the dark, the depths on my thoughts, lost, lonely, looking for clues on what it all means, what is meant for us, for her, for me, is it even meant to be?

My business ideas were moving forward. Dubai was an exciting place to be for me. I had many ideas and they were all being put into a strategic plan to execute over the next few months.

My coach taught me, the speed of implementation will determine your speed of success, and I wanted it to succeed as badly as I wanted to breathe.

I was pushing hard, something I find easy to do, especially when I have a direction and a mapped-out plan of attack. I was in my element; it was game time. I was ready to grow and live by the idea that if you are not growing, you are dying.

I felt more driven than ever, ambitious, focused, determined, willing to do whatever it was going to take, make any sacrifices needed, ready to cut anyone out of my life that was trying to stop me, removing any energy drainers out of my life. This was another lesson my coach taught me, as I asked him during our yacht trip around the Island of Bohol.

My mind had shifted so much into top gear, I felt in a different lane, with more understanding, wisdom, and purpose. My spiritual awareness was increasing rapidly too. It felt like I had matured ten years in just ten days, which sounds hard to write without sounding cocky, but that's the truth! You have to appreciate; I had so many breakthroughs during my trip, it opened up locked doorways I never knew were there. I climbed new levels, and in doing so I was going into the next phase of my life. I was ready for whatever life would throw my way; I knew I was prepared. I knew I could handle it, which is exactly how I needed to feel because I also knew life was going to throw at me hard, I felt that too. The storm will always come and find you, it is not about hiding from it, more about being prepared to withstand the downfall rain and the aggressive winds it brings, then you can deal with the mess after the storm clears and the sun comes back up, which it always does.

My focus had improved, and I was able to blank out the unnecessary and any negative energy coming my way.

Carly and I continued to have endless, pointless conversations on the same topic over and over, like the record was stuck on repeat, constant battles, like each day could potentially lead to war, but I was in military-style mode, tunnel vision on the mission, hyper-focused on my goals to better my future. Anything else that was not congruent with my vision was just background noise at this point.

I chose to spend my energy on my business, building relationships and networking, hustling, grafting, day in day out, like I always did, but this time I pushed a little more because I had more confidence, faith, and belief in myself.

So, I filled my day with work, staying out until late, avoiding the very environment I once felt so relaxed in, I didn't look forward to going home, it felt quite negative there, which we both created.

It seemed to me that Carly was threatened by how fast things were moving, which frightened her, which led her to become very unsupportive to any new ideas I had on how to grow. That's the reason I chose to discuss very few things with her.

I could feel her pulling me down, pulling me back, and I was rebelling, pushing away, which I have always done without anyone trying to stop me.

I am all about positivity, sharing my time with people that enjoy my company, that encourage me, like I do to them, that understand my crazy work ethic and admire it, as I would do in them. I have always avoided being around anyone that doesn't give the same vibration out, maybe not at first, but after some time, after trying to pass mine to them. If they are not willing to change and continue to be negative, I move; I stop trying to help them.

This brought more tension between Carly and I, something I would soon have to address, as we were flying to the U.K. together and sat side by side for eight hours.

We would be attending three weddings whilst we were in the U.K., one on every weekend. The first was Carly's best friend's; Carly was the maid of honor.

The week after was my good friend's, Barney's, and I would get a chance to see all my friends I grew up with.

And, finally, Carly's dad's wedding a week after that. This is the one I was looking most forward to. It had been a while since I have had a few drinks with Carly's dad, uncle, brother, etc., and I just know their wedding would be a fun and a mad one, one to remember if you are lucky enough to.

It would fall on the same time as the F.A. Cup final, Liverpool and Arsenal, and Carly's dad is a MASSIVE Liverpool fan. So halfway through the wedding, they were pulling the big screen down, getting the projector out, lining up a load of chairs to watch the match in the middle of the dance floor.

It would be a very memorable wedding, a perfect way to say goodbye for a few months again.

The trip back to the U.K. would also give us a chance to spend quality time with our families, friends, walk our dog, Chubbz, who stays with my mum. We could hike up the mountains, to reservoirs, forests, and absorb the beautiful surroundings of the green grass of home, my home, there is no place like home.

I could work on a few projects that I have planned and prepare for the biggest day in my life, overcoming my biggest fear and delivering a speech to a thousand people, yikes!

A few days passed and the distance between us was increasing, but it was finally time to face the music or face the silence as we made our way to the airport to try to settle into an uncomfortable flight.

During the flight, we expressed no excitement for our trip, nothing. Just still, dead air between us, completely different from every other flight we've been on, and we have been on so many together. We hardly spoke, there was emptiness between us, stillness filled with unemotional silence.

My wife was very upset, I could feel it in my stomach and as I know she is not one to bring it to the surface, I know that there was a lot down there. She had been upset for some time too, long before I went to my trip away from her, long before the past 12 months when our drift apart started to sail. She was trying to hide it but everyone else by this point could see, well at least I could and it was not nice to see.

She is such a strong, powerful woman, she gives out a lot of energy, sometimes good, sometimes bad, but every time she does, I pick it up easily too, like I am experiencing what she is and I often feel hopeless. How can I help her if she doesn't express her feelings or give in inclination that she wants to share?

On the flight back I pass time reading, watching movies, but I can't seem to distant myself from the scripts in my father's diary that are clear in my thoughts which spark memories I have that are not my own, from someone else's experience that were passed to me on pages. My consciousness is fixated on the deep, meaningful poems inked onto paper that carried my father's battles, struggles, the challenges he faced, ones that made him feel confused with his own sanity, the written poems expressing how other people's opinions haunted him, as they didn't understand his actions or who he had changed into so fast. They didn't understand him nor did they recognize his cry for help.

The pages flick over in my head so fast and play out a movie. As the scenes unfold the story, I hear my father voicing the words over and over.

I can't even remember my father speaking to me or what his voice sounded like, but I was able to hear it as clear as day. It sounded just like my own voice but with a sharper, with a more painful deliverance to it.

I knew these messages would have some importance behind them for the moment I was in and, more importantly, the moments that were to follow!

Chapter 7
The Land of My Father

Touchdown in the UK after eight long hours!

We got off the plane, grabbed our luggage which seemed to be out faster than usual, but we didn't complain as we made our way to the bus stop where we would get on a bus and make a short journey to the depot to pick up our hired car that I pre-booked for us weeks before.

The air was cold and bitter, but it was something I had gotten used to.

It was spring, but the morning felt like winter had come early.

We arrived at the office and I started to fill in the paperwork for the car. That's when I realized I didn't have my wallet with me. I had lost it during our travels, maybe left it on the plane or at the airport, I wasn't sure, but it was alarming, as that's where I stored all my cards. My driving license, Emirates ID, the cash I brought to see us through, everything I needed to finalize the contract on the car that would get us back to Wales from London, drive us around to see our family and back again when the trip ended.

They couldn't help us at the depot, we had no option but to go back to the airport, check to see if it was handed-in, if not, to find another way back to Wales.

We went around all the car-hiring companies to see if we could hire without my driving license and bank card, but they all refused.

We were just about to jump on the bus which we knew would have taken three times as long, as nothing was straightforward with public transport, I somehow remembered the 16 characters to my driving license, which I don't even remember seeing. We were lucky to find a company that would allow us to use this along with a card that wasn't in my name, Carly's card. The downside was that the car was double the price of what I had already paid and that was the cheapest model.

This seemed to spark an unsettling argument in the middle of the airport between us. An argument over money, that was a first; we never did this before. It was petty because to me it didn't matter who paid; money was money and we needed to use it.

We were not on the same level of thinking. I got frustrated partly because I had already paid for one car that we couldn't drive.

She stormed off, disappearing into the crowd of Heathrow's busy airport, leaving me with no money, no card, no license, just my suitcases and the mood I was left in.

I sat in Starbucks, assuming she was on the bus on her way back to Wales, puzzled by how I would get to Wales. The fact I had no battery for my phone made it worse, but I was kind of glad, as if it was the icing on the cake, like I had a stronger reason to do my own thing. I had to, but I guess I wanted to.

I wasn't that concerned that she had left me, I didn't think much about whether she would come back or not. It didn't bother me; it was her choice and out of my control, I just had to pick myself up from another situation I never planned but had to get out of.

A short time later, she returned with a coffee for us both, which I guess was her way of saying sorry behind the stubbornness she wore. In that moment, we both knew it was the start of a challenging week together, but little did we know how challenging it would be.

The diary

Dear father,

Please keep me off the doctor's drugs also because I believe that with you and only you, I can be redeemed from my sins through the repentance.

I don't think that I am mad, but I have had my mind damage and my soul hunt.

This was caused through my own wrongdoing. If I would take your drugs, then I could fall again into temptation, so I am afraid of the drugs in case they change me again.

My quest in life is for my own salvation because I want to be made right in the sight of the lord.

Please allow me a little time without drugs to see if I can.

I drove for miles until the concrete city slowly disappeared and we were welcomed by mountains of freshness.

The change in contrast was so evident as we made our way to Merthyr Tydfil, the small working-class town of South Wales.

Once it was the heart of the country many years ago, home of the ironworks that distributed to many parts of Britain too, home to me and my father. But like we were experiencing, nothing seems to last forever, hearts that are remembered for their title sometimes die.

It didn't have the respected power it had during 1995 when it was recognized as the capital of Wales. Back then it had so much opportunity for work, people would travel from all over the UK just to make a living. Now the streets were filled with people living to work.

I am an immensely proud Welshman; I love Wales. I feel humbled by my roots and the amazing memories I have embedded from growing up in this part of the world. It has helped mold and shape my character. It has built strength and taught me so many valuable lessons.

Unfortunately, it's also home to a lot of people who are struggling to find their way, that seem lost. There is a lot of violence, crime, and drugs. Some people are so fearful to go out at night, to go out without leaving the light on, because when they do, the chances of someone breaking in is high. It's the sad truth, and if anyone that reads this gets annoyed, then they are in denial, or loyal, and defending, fighting for the home, which I will do too, come-on Wales.

It can be like a spider's web; it tends to hold people in, holding them back from seeing what is out there, forcing many to stand still, watching the world go by, feeling like they can make a move forward, so why try. It is almost like the story of the Elephant and the stick, which is one of my favorites.

This is not the case for everybody of course, but a large percent of the population. I know because I am one of them too.

There is a lot of negativity and lack of support for those daring enough to express their desires with others, who think ambitiously, chase their goals, and follow their dreams.

Often such talk would be nothing more than entertainment for many. It would be humorous and comical listening to someone talk about how they are going to change the world. I guess that is how it is in many other parts of the world too, but I wasn't born there. I am just sharing my experience from the world I was born into, from the roots of my perceptive. And as the legendary Steve Jobs once said, those that are crazy enough to think they can change the world, are the ones that do! So, I admire anyone with a passion to do something HUGE, especially when they are confident in their own ability, that formula right there is exactly what is needed to do just that.

I will always be proud of where I come from and aspire to create positive change. One of my biggest goals is to guide the younger generation, help them find their purpose and go after it, to lead by an example, lead from the front. I am inspired to inspire, focused on getting in a position of power, authority, and recognition, to one day, someday, go back and help those in my community, the community I was born and raised in. To help them see the light and believe in themselves. But before I can confidently do that, I must achieve greatness first, and I am far from there yet. I have so much more to learn, more goals to set, more to accomplish, more to understand. I have to find my way, find myself before I can convince others to believe in me. I have to convince myself!

I have always enjoyed going home, my real home, the home where all my true friends are and my loving family. Visiting the places, I hung out at, which reminds me of my childhood. The place always sparked deep, meaningful memories of past experiences that would remind me of where I came from, where I have been, where I am, and where I am going.

This time, for the first time, it feels different. I feel like I no longer belonged, like I am an outsider or one that may not be welcomed. I feel a little judged and distant from everyone, which I know I am creating too, which is more to do with the state I am in and have been in.

So much has happened in my life since the last time I visited. I too feel as different as others view me, judging myself, my thoughts, and my actions or lack of.

I am a lone wolf, have been for some time. I spend a lot of time on my own, which I enjoy. I am very selective to who I share my time with. I know the one person that has always got my back is me, and I am the only person I can really rely on.

My circle of trusted people is very small and tight, but it was becoming tighter. There are not many people I can open up to, receive support on my ideas that will welcome the change in my cognitive ability, new mindset, consciousness expansion, even in my newfound spirituality.

But seeing people I know for some time, the still many conversations with gaps of silence, awkward moments, allowed me to see, we all changed!

But it felt as though I was on a different page, no longer on the same page as I was, the page many were still on.

I was adapting to the new environment I had placed myself in and it was far from the one I came from. The change was so rapid in me, it was hard for anyone to understand or accept. Many whispered behind my back that I tried to ignore, but it's like they had become so loud I just couldn't.

"He has become so career-driven and selfish in his ways!" I would imagine them say, which echoed in my ear, even when I tried to sleep.

Was I going mad, or were they?

All this confusion made me upset, frustrated, annoyed, but also happy I had changed but for the better, for the better of us all, a cocktail of emotions to sip on fueled me for the journey that was ahead.

And I know my goal was bigger than just me; it was to help everyone, that includes them too.

There is one person that has always been on my side, supporting me, standing against anyone that didn't, and she was on the other side of the fence too. I felt so lonely at times, and what's worse is it's like she no longer likes the person I am or the more like the one I am becoming.

I remember thinking, *What's wrong with them?*

The dairy

Why can't they see?

It's just me.

I am here.

I am just a little wiser, smarter, and brighter!

I don't get it, I am a harder worker; I work extremely hard.

I admit I can be a hard work too, but I am not a bad guy.

I never wish bad on anyone. I am just me, kind and generous, often putting others before me!

The thoughts of confusion saddened me. I was tilting to the floor, bending at my knees, to the point of giving up, giving in, jumping on a plane back to my new home, until the fire started in me.

It started to heat me up and boil my blood and make me a little angry, wood for the fire to burn, I call it.

I don't need anyone anyway.

I can push toward my goals, my ambitious, with or without the support or the approval from anyone else other than me!

The first wedding number showed up, Carly's best friend.

Besides Carly, her auntie, Liz, and her uncle, Dai, the bride and groom were the only people I knew in the venture. I was often left with Liz and Dai, as Carly was doing her part, entertaining the guests and making sure the bride was having a good day.

We got into a disagreement about the fact that she wanted to do something different with her job, something she had been talking about for so long, but she was making excuses and procrastinating. I gave her my opinion and advice, but she got very defensive and very upset. She stormed off for the second time, leaving me sitting on a table in the middle of the bar with uncle Dai, her auntie followed her up to her room.

Dai and I had a good chat, man to man. We always have great conversations. He understood where I was coming from and my intention to help her go in the direction she wanted. He told me that he often felt the same with Liz and that she and Carly were very similar in their ways.

Liz was like a mother figure to Carly, but they were more like sisters, which was beautiful to see.

The next few days were a balancing act of emotional eruptions. I was too busy to confront them, keeping busy too, distracting myself from the truth and masking it from others. Well, trying to at least, but it was obvious to see, you cannot hide your true feelings.

I would spend the day at the coffee shop, checking in on my online clients, making sure they were still receiving my support even whilst I was away. I would take calls from there, arrange meeting on Skype and meet there with any friends before heading off to the gym to vent my frustration and release the tension I was swallowing, digesting and storing, ready to be released, like a caged beast. The iron always carried me through emotional challenges, that's why I married the weights room!

The gym is my therapy, my happy place, my sanctuary. My first love and I will always love it. It never judges me. It always welcomes me back no matter how the previous day was.

The weight room literally saved me. Took me from the road I was heading down and showed me a new direction, a better route. It was somewhere I could turn all the negative energy around that I felt within me and channel it into a positive outcome. It helped change the way I looked, the way I looked at myself and everything else. It introduced me to the world of bodybuilding, and I found my passion, a way to express my art, creating an image I saw in my mind, using the weights to mold and sharp my body until it was ready to display.

It allowed me to create that vision I saw, the one I got to present on stage in front of hundreds of people, showcasing the masterpiece I worked tirelessly on, one that was fueled by so many emotions, one that told a story of one's journey, one's life. An artist would paint on canvas, use finer brushes to illustrate the detail, bring the image to life and display their piece of art in a museum where it would be showcased for many years. But me, I am a bodybuilder by heart, and a display my art through the building of my body.

My mother often said that my father's problem was that his art was his first love and that he too would use it as therapy. He couldn't leave it alone. He would always return to it. That is likely to be one of the reasons they started drifting in the first place.

He changed as time went by. He got so consumed in his passion, in his artwork, that he lost sight of the people around him.

I once thought the biggest difference between my chosen art form and my fathers' was that I chose the painful route. As my art is created only after walking the path that travels through severe pain, but he had walked it too.

He had faced so much pain to bring his artwork to life, the pain of losing his family, and leading to the loss of his life, which hopefully ends the suffering.

My dad was so ambitious. My mother supported his dreams and goals.

They moved to Hereford, away from Wales, to further his career in art, to study at the university there. I was one year old. He wanted to improve the life for us all, using his passion to drive up, up-skilling his talent to navigate us. We were starting fresh in a place where people were more like-minded as him and on a similar path of their own. My mum didn't see how consuming all your time and energy into a passion that was not bringing money home or food on the table was a ticket to financial freedom. His obsession became too much, so she builds up the courage and she left him. Alone he stayed, without his family, his son, and step-daughter, my sister.

He was left with his artwork and the painful thoughts that were brewing.

My mum has a psyche gift, I think we all do, but she seems to see a little further ahead than most. Maybe she saw something beyond the eyes could see. What the path he was on would lead to, the loss of his mind, in the eyes of others, and eventually the death of him!

On May, the 9th, 1999, five years after my mum walked away from my dad, never to return, never to give it another chance, John Kaler, my father, lost his life whilst trying to keep his passion alive. He died tragically and bravely whist rescuing his paintings from the flames he died in.

He had woken up in his flat and it was on fire, there was thick smoke everywhere, but he managed to get out. He saved his pet bird that was in the flat with him, he placed it on the balcony. They were both safe, breathing in fresh air.

He went back into the flat, he collapsed from the lack of oxygen created by thick carbon rich smoke that surrounded him and died! He would be later found lying to rest peacefully behind the door.

He went back in to save the visons he brought to life, the life of his art work, his paintings. But nobody really knows the reason why a man would turn back around and walk into a place that was so hard to see your hand in front of your face, a place that had no clear way out, a one-way ticket!

Maybe it was fate, and not tragedy, and he knew it.

What I do know, after reading his diary, is that he wasn't in the right state of mind. He was confused, depressed, questioning his faith and belief, but what he was sure of is that the Devil was after him and his life was coming to a close!

Which I find so bizarre, and never knew this about my dad, I don't think anyone did!

But did my mum? Did she sense some sort of warning with her psychic ability to see into the future?

Did she see the potential route he was steering toward, a journey to an early grave? That intuition you cannot explain but can't ignore.

What's ironic is that the very passion that fueled my father's life, lead to the death of him.

But what is even more ironic is I can see my own life tell a similar story, but to where will I be led is the question?

Could my passion be the death of me?

Would the decision to sacrifice anything to achieve my goals include sacrificing my life?

Blinded by the truth, even when others are pointing it out.

This script from the past carries with it new meaning for me now.

It has great significance on my present and my progressive future.

The ideas that lead to many clues.

A reason to look deep and unravel the truth.

I have never met anyone like me, my father is the closest person that resembles that who I am.

And I am his!

He has taught me so much teaching.

Learnt lessons from his life, helping me learn my own.

He has shown me how we can still connect.

How we can be felt from the other side if we strive to leave a legacy, a gift to pass to our child.

There are many people I have in my life that have also helped guide me and steer me into the right direction.

Another man I look up to is James Llewellyn. He is one of my good friends, one of my mentors, my coaches.

He has taught me so much, not just about bodybuilding or how to peak for a contest but also on how to handle the tough times in life, the curveballs life throws. He has been there for many years, guiding me, supporting me, correcting me, and telling me off if I am out of line with my actions.

I was always a big fan of James for many years, as he is one of the most recognized bodybuilders from Wales. I read about him in all the magazines, bought his DVDs, watched him guest-posing on stage, and followed his YouTube channel.

It's hard to believe the relationship we have now and how connected we are.

His birthday was approaching and one we planned for a while.

We would stay down in Swansea to celebrate with some drinks, food, and stay the night. Carly and I booked the hotel and paid for the meal as a gift and to show much appreciation to someone we have for him and his wife, who are both dear friends of ours.

It turned out to be a bit of a disaster in the end!

The day started bright, like every one, but then comes the cold, darkness of the night. The alcoholic drinks started to flow, a chance to drown any sorrows, and gave a little bit of Dutch courage, enough to create a murder on the dance floor.

We were with two other couples, both of which were by this time showing affection publicly, another benefit getting drunk, lack of care. They were, kissing, hugging, dancing, having fun, which become a little awkward for me and my wife. It was not just because of the fact we had been living in a Muslim country for long; another to not dare displace anything more than a little kiss, but we were slightly disconnected from each other. Our relationship was not how it was when we had left Wales either.

It was so clear for our friends to see, we had become so different, how we were not the same, not sharing the same joy as we once did.

The more shots we seemed to neck back, the more intense the situation got, which sparked a lot of seeded emotions, anger, pain, and aggression.

Carly started getting aggressive in her tone, in her actions too.

She always did get a little violent when she was drunk, nothing that would lead to any reasonable harm, but still this time I was not going to stand for it.

I deserved more. I finished my drink and walked away. I went to a quite spot in the town and spent a little time on my own, removing myself from the situation I was in, but didn't want to be.

I gathered my thoughts, cleared my head, I was back feeling in a positive way, so I returned. It was mostly to show my respect to my coach, friends, but also to show Carly that I am stronger than what she may think, and to prove to myself that I can get through these moments because I knew there would be a lot more to come.

We got back to the hotel and she said some nasty words, which made me feel terrible.

I knew it was partly the drink talking, it can encourage anyone to talk with no filter, but what she said really hurt, as I trusted my wife's opinion on anyone, even me.

The next morning, we had breakfast and sat down with our friends that loved us both so we could apologize for the evening. They weren't offended at all; they were very understanding, but a little concerned.

James said to us both that we should really think about where we will go from there, because we may not only lose our marriage but lose our best friend. Then he said, "Maybe you already have".

He suggested to spend some time apart. Time to think clearly about what we really wanted, then we could decide what.

We took his advice and discussed our thoughts with each other on the drive back to Merthyr where we would get ready for wedding number two.

As we start getting older, late 20s into early 30s, we don't see our friends we were brought up with often at all. In fact, the only time we get together is for some big weddings or a funeral. Which is a little sad, but I understand that everyone is on their own journey, path, and it's kind of "it is what it is", you can't stay in Neverland forever, Peter Pan had to grow up.

That is why we must enjoy the time we do get, when that time presents.

Regardless of the situation that brought us back together, even if it was a death, it is a celebration of life, the life that was lived, and the lives still living.

Barney's wedding was in a huge castle in the middle of nowhere. It was surrounded by nothing but breathtaking views, mountains with great peaks, endless green landscape that went on further than to what looked like the end of the world. It was like the garden of Eden from a far, colors flowing from one to another, rows of flowers positioned perfectly in the beds that they rooted in, it felt so peaceful and organic, especially after living in the desert where Dubai was made.

A special place, a perfect place to say your vows to the person you only hope to spend your life with.

I am to spend some good old time with my friends. It had been years since we got together. It seemed I knew everyone there and they knew me.

All my close friends I grew up with, all of which were mostly married by now. My circle was always tight but was once a lot bigger than now.

Carly and I were getting on great, even though less than 12 hours ago we were like enemies. We were spending quality time together, and it didn't feel like we did because we had to, or because we were expected to.

During the evening, I was having a beer with a close friend, Gwyn Williams, a guy I have so much respect for. He is extremely hardworking, a very successful, an incredible dad, and a loving family man. He has all the attributes I think build a strong male character and role model to a son.

I opened up to him about my true feeling, about what we're going through and the fact that I have accepted the truth. We are no longer compatible; we are different, on different paths, holding each other back, and I don't think we can make it.

He came close enough to look deep into my eyes and really talk to me. He said, "Listen, that woman over there loves you like no other. She has been there for you from day one when you had nothing. She has stuck by you through the bad days, not just the good."

I felt the honest tone of his voice. I respected his words of wisdom and we continued chatting in confidence with each other, which neither of us had to ask for but knew it was a safe place between two brothers.

I talked about how I felt Carly is not supporting my desired goals, that I realized my potential and I wanted to fulfill it. I wanted to climb the mountain top and achieve my ambitions, and I was willing to sacrifice anything, the today for tomorrow, the people that are holding me back.

What Gwyn said to me next will stick in my mind for a long time. It sparked something deep inside me, made me understand my life. The real reason why I never feel satisfied, undeserving of enjoying my achievements. Why I am always looking for the next challenge, seeking something bigger, something better. The reason why my wife, my family, my friends are not giving me the support I feel I deserve, maybe they can see it too, and perhaps they don't condone it as a way of living.

He looked me in the eye and talked to my soul, "I know exactly how you feel, buddy. I understand, but you know what the problem is?"

He paused and gave me a moment to think, which stimulated my curiosity into his thoughts, my pupils opened up wide.

"You are so focused on the future; you are forgetting to enjoy the present."

I thought about what he said over and over that night.

And I realized I was, but isn't that what it takes to be successful I questioned.

My life is for a bigger purpose than just me and the present, it was for the future of so many others, that is my sacrifice, the cross I carry.

My father taught me more about life, after his death, than when he was living.

Where others see sacrifice with no meaning, I see it as an exchanging of time, the passing of ages.

The days that followed this wedding Carly went to stay over her aunts to spend quality time with her family before we went back to Dubai. This was also to give us space we need, take advice that was passed to us by our friends. We thought it may bring us closer, but I am not if anything other than keep us apart.

I just kept busy, arranging things, ready to kick off as soon as I landed. Working on some marketing ideas and finalizing all the costs, and arrange meeting with potential business partners to a workshop I was creating.

Which would put us on the map and be more recognized fitness professionals in Dubai.

Everyone deals with things different. Some people collapse under pressure, give up, give in. I use it as a fuel to create more movement. I turn negative into positive and use it to my advantage. It's how I have always delt with life's tragedies, it's what has always gotten me through tough times.

We had made it through two weddings and onto the third. So many conversations with the family about our relationship, where we were going, and how we could resolve this problem.

Advice on how to get it back on track, suggestions to see a counselor to help us with our marriage. Advice to spend less time working, less time in work, which was for me, as apparently, I should take my foot off the peddle. I was pressing down hard, have done for some time, and was going to continue to do so. A little stuck in my way, but a way I enjoyed it, so I never really listen too much of the suggestions like this, as it was creating a life I dreamt of.

We arrived at the wedding we both looked forward to for so long and it was exactly how we had imagined it. Nothing fancy, just a good time spent with some good people, drinking, and sharing stories from the past, good music, good food, good company.

When the footy came on, it was crazy, but in a great way. We had so much fun together, everyone did. We danced, we sang, we celebrated, we hugged, and we kissed. It was perfect and a perfect way to say goodbye to everyone.

At the end of the night, Carly's dad took me to one side and said, "Look after her for me, buddy." He often said this, but in the current situation, with what we were going through, it felt a little different and had more meaning to it, I felt more responsible for her happiness and wellbeing.

The next morning, we said our goodbyes to all our family and loved ones, which was an emotional time because we knew it would be a long time before we'd see them again, and by the time we did, we didn't know if we would still be a couple. We made our way off to London, from where we would be flying back to Dubai the next evening, where we would be picking up where we left off, wherever that was, we had been so caught up in confusion, pleasure, and pain.

But before we did, we would celebrate the birthday of a very special woman in my life. A woman that has helped me be the man I am today. I made a vow to myself that I wouldn't let anyone, or anything upset the day, or my mood. I was going to forget the past, abandon the future, just to be fully present in moment and live it as if it was the last. The goal was to make sure she felt like the angel she is, that I made her feel special on her special day. The day that is all about her, her birth, her existence, her life, and the lives she has brought more life to.

The date was 2nd of June 2019, Carly's 28th birthday. I had planned a surprise for this for some time, one that I knew she would be excited about.

It came at the right time for her too, for us. It was exactly what we needed. To spend quality time together with no external distractions, past, or forecast, just the now!

I booked the same, exact same hotel that I booked her with seven years before on her 21st birthday, and that as well as this time was a surprise.

The place has a special place in our hearts, like the memories of each other we have.

It was overlooking Westminster Bridge, Big Ben, and the London Eye, a perfect location and view. The difference was that this time, I booked the best room in the hotel. It was so much bigger, with incredible views from the huge windows that your eyes gravitated to as soon as you walked in.

I also booked a reservation at the best restaurant in London. Seated at the highest floor rotating a full 360-degrees every hour with breath taken panoramic experience. A perfect place to plan our tour for the next day around this historical city.

We got on so well, better than we had done for months, we had a perfect time. Where this would lead, we did not know, nor did we care, it was not a concern. We were happy, with genuine infectious smiles on our faces. We felt the love and it was felt by others too.

Some say that time can be a healer, and when you are broken down, the only way is up.

Were we healing, moving to a better future together, or did we have more breaking to go through, and moving further apart?

The diary

O God, let me dream a lovely dream.

O God, let me see a lovely scene.

Let me forget the sadness of where I have been.

I dared to be judge others.

Of this, I am guilty.

How dare I judge others when I have broken every commandment except kill!

Yes, I have done this in the past, but past is the past I thought.

Magic, if it really exists, should only be good.

O God, good has its operative.

Chapter 8
Facing My Fears

I often wondered, why do we let fear stop us taking action and moving forward?

Fear is something we all experience, some of us lean into it, but most of us lean away.

But what is it, is it the fear of failure, the fear of success, fear of embarrassment, regret, resentment, fear of dying, fear of living, that makes this universal experience shared by so many, a daunting thought of a potential future?

Fear is not the truth, it lives in our minds, it is only one outcome of so many possibilities, often enough, it's not even logical outcome, yet many believe the lie, and it prisons us from escaping the confinement of our doubts.

We build an imaginary wall, place it in front of our desires, and ambitions, which we then allow to stop us going forward. Because the unknown is scary, uncertain, uncomfortable. The mind has a safety mechanism that protects us, keeps us safe, in our comfortable place, highlights all the hazards, and stops us taking risks.

The mind doesn't like change, any situation we are in that could lead to change is disruptive, the actions take place in the mind to stop the body acting.

The mind is what controls the body; the body does not control the mind. We are hardwired like this, that have been passed down and came with us. And for reason, the survival of our species, as it is for all other creatures on Earth. But we humans are uniquely different! We are curious, we want to know more, explore more, test our capabilities, push to our limits and find new ways to push beyond. It's the very reason why we have evolved at such a rapid rate and adapted to many different environments over the centuries. Our ability to push forward and take risks, as hard as they may be to take, gambling life, sacrificing it, it is what sets us apart from all we know.

Many of us live for this, addicted to the game, the adrenaline rush felt when we are challenging our emotional state, testing our body, risking it all, living on the edge of our capabilities and far from comfort!

This is what separates the great from the norm, the ability to see fear as a progressing stepping stone to a higher level. Moving in the same direction without holding back, overcoming fear to climb to the top, focusing on what the future will bring from the challenging present.

The pituitary gland is responsible for triggering the release of adrenaline from the adrenal glands into the bloodstream to cause a reaction, the flight-or-fight response which is part of the endocrine system, along with many other hormones released at different times.

During a time when we are fearful, to the extreme, like in a life-or-death situation, it's needed for our survival. Some will freeze, cower, run, and hide away to be safe, and some on the other hand will stand up and prepare to fight, and even run towards the whatever is feared. The same hormone that is released can lead to completely different outcomes, outcome from personal beliefs, that have been embedded from past experiences or a similar nature.

I welcome fear, I love to challenge myself to take action on what is standing between me and my goals. I seek fear because I know what it leads to. I still get extremely nervous and anxious. By facing my fears and overcoming them, I have gained move confidence in facing more, which is always a bigger challenge than the last, with bigger risks but bigger rewards.

The fear of public speaking was so far the biggest fear I had faced, and knew I had to. Like I have always done, I chose to dive in the deep end with the sharks, so you not only have to learn to swim, but you have to learn fast, and swim faster.

Standing up and speaking in front of a small group was a fear, but what did I do, stand in front of almost a thousand people and deliver a speech!

I had to do it, I needed to, to get to the next level in my career, the next stage in my life, to give me a new story to tell, an opportunity to motivate every person that had the same fear, which is so many. People fear public speaking more than they fear death, it is our survival instinct, glaring unfamiliar eyes means danger.

There was no fear about remembering my words, I was not worried at all, I had practiced them over and over, I could recite them in my sleep. In fact, I was dreaming about the day before it came. I worked so hard to ensure I could deliver a message, improved my tonality, my pitch throw; I wanted to create an impact and send a message to the masses.

I was dressed to impress with a new tailored suit, polished shoes, a J.T. Foxx tie and clean shave. I was looking successful, confident, and I knew I would be respected enough to be listened to just by my appearance.

I didn't have much time to prepare, especially with what we were going from, the mental battle, trial, tribulations, and separations, but I don't use that as an excuse and throw in the towel. The situation taught me a valuable lesson; I don't need that much time at all to prepare for such speeches. I have a gift, and my ability to zone in, push away distractions, hyper focus on my chosen tasks. The only fear I had was my anxiety, controlling nerves onstage as hundreds of people sit in silence and stare at me, listening to every vibration that comes from my mouth, which was amplified by the surround sound speakers the hi-tech microphone attached to my collar was wired too.

That morning I woke up earlier than my alarm, which I always did when I was excited about the day ahead. It was a beautiful morning, I went for a walk over to the park close to my home, did my morning march through the paths and went through the series of positive affirmations I did every morning, this time it felt different. I felt different. The words seemed to lift my spirit; I understood the true essence of each word more clearly. I would usually say them to feel better, but this time I was feeling better by saying them, it sparked light inside me, I felt like a magnet to positivity. It was something I never experienced.

The march turned into a glide. Like I was floating on air, weightless. I felt air in my breath, the beat in my heart. The trail of thoughts of awareness the way inside out. I slowed my pace so I could just pause for a moment. I took a deep gentle breath in, sat down, and felt the living grass beneath wrap around my skin and comfort me.

I bathed in a river of abundance that was flowing to me, through me. My eyes closed to experience everything in a new sense of exploration. The perfect harmony and rhythm of peace blissfully igniting my gratitude for being. I could hear and feel everything, vibrations were carried by waves of love, from points of awareness.

The birds chirping, tweeting, communicating with each other from all around, leaves on the trees softly blowing in the very calm air that seemed to carry a little wind, like a slight echo. The harmless buzzing of bees around me and the flapping of their tiny wings as they flew past me. An incredible gift, beautifully powerful with no ego at all, just clarity. I was living in the present moment, soaking up the energy that was flooding into my hands, I could feel every vibration of life. I was a pool of power, building up to the point of overflowing. My body began to vibrate, I felt hot, but it wasn't uncomfortable or disruptive to my calm Zen state of mind; it was inviting, and I felt immensely powerful.

It made sense, I was aware that my thoughts sparked my emotions, energy in motion. I realized that this is my reality, it is my world, and I am in control, I can absorb only want I desire, choose what I let in, what I receive, and what I push out. I knew that this day and every day that follows was going to have more meaning. It was going to be incredible. It was going to change my life forever.

I understand that every day that was before this day was just to get to this one and the only opportunity I was about to take.

I went back home, had breakfast, got dressed, and made my way to the venue. I was ecstatically charged with rich currency and ready to share with others.

I was so excited but also extremely nervous of what was to come when I took the stage. I was soon called up to deliver my speech and take the opportunity to overcome my fear. I took a deep breath in, closed my eyes, put my hand on my heart, thanked my father as he helped me during my preparation, and for watching over me. I softened my lips with the wetness from my tongue, opened my eyes, relaxed my jaw, and let the words float out of me for the next five minutes as I delivered a speech on overcoming fear and taking action, the very thing I was doing up there.

My speech

"What I realized is that when we want something so bad, we literally can't stop thinking about it. Then usually the opportunity presents, but we get fearful and anxious, which is something we all face. But if we just take action and say yes, if we just do it and don't quit, we will be one step closer to what we truly want.

"The biggest obstacle we will ever face in life is that fearful wall we place in front of ourselves that tries to stop us moving forward.

"Four weeks ago, my biggest fear was standing in front of an audience, speaking. Whilst in the Philippines, J.T. gave me the

opportunity to stand here and give a speech today.

"Christian, you're not prepared.

What if you can't remember your words?

What if they can't understand your accent?

Christian, you have never spoken in front of more than 30 people.

What are you doing, don't do it, say no.

"I took action and I said yes without letting fear stop me or without coming up with any reason why I shouldn't.

I'm Christian Williams, and I'm thankful for every one of you here today listening to me and being a part of my beautiful journey, which will be a combination of excitement, opportunities, fear, and of course, the most important, acting.

"And I encourage each and every one of you, if you ever let fear hold you back in the past and you have come here today, you take action, you say yes."

This is the last two minutes of my speech that I presented at the J.T. Foxx Mega Speaker event.

What an honor it was, speaking at an event that was to inspire the listeners to become a speaker. I loved it. It came so naturally. People came up to me during the break asking for if they can take a picture with me. It was so overwhelming. There were so many people inspired and motivated to take action and get over their fear of speaking. I knew it would lead to so much more; the opening of new doorways to new beginnings, ones that would direct my path into a better future.

It seems miraculous, it takes one moment, one opportunity, one chance to act and your life could explode, and mine was about to from this.

I have had many moments in my life where one decision lead to a completely different outcome from the one I was heading towards. Like butterfly effect affects us all, some positive, some not so, but that's a matter of choice too, depending on how you look at any given situation.

When I was 15 years old, I was walking home from school, it was the last day of the term. What would follow was the six weeks summer holiday, that would lead into the last year of comprehensive school. I was very upset about the way someone said I looked.

Earlier that afternoon a girl that I had a crush on, and I were sitting together as we often did. She threw a pencil at me as a joke, it hit me in my chest. I said, "Ow, my chest!" She started laughing and said, "Your boobs you mean, they're bigger than mine." I laughed with her, but she was right.

I never felt insecure about my weight, nor did it affect me. I wasn't a fat kid, but I was overweight. I was a junk-food junky, and the result of overeating on bad food turned me into a little chunk.

I knew I needed to change; I was getting fat.

I decided to take action that day, I decided to change. It was time to stop eating any food I considered bad for me, cut out all the fizzy pop, only drink water and only eat meat, salads, veg, and fruit. Time to go running every day. Do press ups and sit ups in my bedroom. I was determined and committed. I had to return to school six weeks later, transformed.

I followed the plan to the T, didn't deviate once, and I returned to school 6 weeks transformed. From chubby food addict, to a shredded fitness fanatic.

I was the most-talked-about pupil in school; the change was shocking. Everyone was shocked. I was shocked. I never expected that one moment could create such an impact on how different I looked, felt.

My mother questioned if I was taking drugs because of how fast I dropped the weight.

It allowed me to see what I can achieve by focusing my 100% attention on my desired goal.

There was so much positive movement from flicking that switch.

I was made captain of my local football and rugby team; all my academics improved fast; I was getting more attention from the girls and I liked it. I was addicted and there was no going back.

The life I was led into was the one I am living today.

Standing up onstage, speaking in front of so many, taking action on another goal, was another defining moment, just like when I was 15. I could feel it, I knew it, and trust in my intuition.

After I came offstage, I looked at my Carly and I said, "They want me to speak tomorrow in Abu Dhabi too."

She said, "They asked you, did they?"

I replied, "Not yet, but they are going to."

We came back from the break to sit and listen, and learn from J.T. He mentioned he was going to Abu Dhabi the next day and was offering someone a chance to get free coaching on the way if they were to take him. Hundreds of people put their hand up to snap the opportunity. I was one of them too. He looked at me and said, "Christian, you can take me. You are one of the family"! A few minutes after, I received a text from one of his team, giving me the instructions, time, and location to pick him from and drop him too. I looked at Carly and said, "See, I told you,".

The next morning, I got to deliver my speech in front of 500 people in Abu Dhabi, but this time it felt completely different. There were no nerves, no anxiety, no fear. There was just pure awareness of everyone in front of me engaged, watching, and listening. Well, some were not interested, but this got me more excited and enthusiastic to try and win them all over. It began to feel like a game to me, one I was trying to win. It felt like I was meant to be, meant for me, my purpose. It felt as if all the times I had been onstage before as a bodybuilder was building my confidence and experience being onstage so I could one day stand up and speak. Speak and encourage, inspire, motivate, bring life to other people, instead of using my body, using my choice of words and delivered by my voice. To help others action taken, and go after their goals. Under the same umbrella, a goal is a goal.

When I came of stage, I knew it was time to face something else that had been on my mind for some time. I wouldn't call it fear, but I knew it would be an uncomfortable experience, and, like fear, a stepping stone.

Carly and I tried to make it work, but it was becoming too challenging to keep trying, we were failing.

Coming home was getting tougher, I would often sit in the car for 30-plus minutes, collecting my thoughts before I went inside. Staying out late working in a coffee shop, as they stay open until late in Dubai. Using my time to do anything I could to feed me with positivity, and to distract me from the truth.

I just didn't feel the same anymore, which was confusing. I didn't understand why I felt that way and why I didn't feel much at all.

Carly was everything I ever wanted, and she made me feel wanted. She is attractive, beautiful, on the inside too. Such a kind, loving woman, I did love her, but we were not the same, our relationship was dying.

I was even more confused when Carly started acting completely different to what she ever did. Cooking all my meals, cleaning, prepping my clothes for work, and being overly nice to me. She would text me in the day, show me affection and attention, almost too much, like it was staged, forced, false, like she was pretending to be somebody she was not, someone she thought I wanted. But this was a little off putting, I didn't want her to be anything but her, not mold herself to fit my needs. It just didn't feel natural, it didn't feel like her.

I was scratching my head, living in a bubble, waiting for it to burst and flood my mind with the truth. I was consumed by my thoughts as I watched the people on the outside dance like monkey in a movie, like puppets on a string.

I found myself spending more time alone but that wasn't helping the situation. It seemed to just cause more irritation between us as we were drifting apart.

I must admit, I did start missing her though, missing someone, I needed energy more than ever. Every time I would get any excitement about going home, I would get home and all I felt was numb, empty, and negative. So many eruptions between us, especially knowing that I was happier spending time with other people, or time on my own.

My mind was working overtime; it was not a nice state to be in. I was struggling to focus on my goals. I saw distractions and obstacles everywhere. My mind was chaotic, I needed help but didn't know who to turn to.

The people I looked up to that were successful speakers, businessmen, champions, and leaders, and what they said helped them deal with their struggles, stresses that the path to success brought was meditation.

They all claimed that meditation helped them gain more clarity and more focus in their life.

It was something I wanted to practice for a while. I always felt the urge to give it a go but never got around to it, didn't have the time or at least couldn't justify spending time doing nothing but thinking, or trying not to even think!

But now was the time, I needed to find peace within as I was living in an internal battle, going to war every day.

You could say I stumbled across meditation; I saw it as a way out of my cluttered mind. I had no idea about the journey it would take me on and how it would connect me to areas of my mind I didn't even know were there, locked, waiting to be opened and allow me to receive more consciousness, enhancing my senses, allowing me to see there is meaning to everything, there is other dimensions, realities, a higher intelligence we can all tap into to gain more wisdom and understanding through the codes the connect being.

Chapter 9
My Therapy

The days led into weeks, as the minutes of each day seemed to dissolve from my numb existence during the struggles I was facing. Tension was building up, mainly because I wasn't dealing with my external problems which were buried internally under layers of toughness.

It seemed people I thought I never started turning against me. I needed to wake up, stop acting stupid, becoming crazy, they said.

I will end up with nothing but loneliness, penalizing me for chasing a dream, stating that I was pushing people away to do so.

I was as though I am experiencing many things my father was going through, what he wrote about in his diary, the very things I did not understand, and almost in the sequence to how he did. The pain, confusion, questioning whether I am becoming selfish, obsessed with passion, questioning if it is me or them that has gone crazy.

I never felt this way in my life. I was in a turmoil, suffering with the reality I was prisoned in my mind, trapped in my thoughts, alone, crying for help on the inside but too stubborn to bring it to the surface where it could be seen, instead locking it down deep.

It was hard to find someone to talk to, to express my true thoughts and feeling, with no judgement of them. Someone I could get the stress off my chest and lift the weight off my shoulders. Every time I spoke the truth, it would hurt, hurt others as well as me, it would lead to so much eruption. It was not worth the aftermath. I always choose to stay in silence, bottling it all up, but knowing a storm is brewing inside, and there will eventually be a lot of rain. I felt so judged for my behavior, and selfish actions, I was even starting to judge myself; I looked different, and I was looked at differently.

I knew I needed to be stronger than before and knew that all the previous challenges I faced were lessons that were preparing me for the big tests.

I was weak and vulnerable. I could see the cracks that needed fixing, the chips that needed filling, and the axe needed sharpening.

My actions were persuaded by other people's feeling. I was making choices that more aligned with what other people wanted, and I had been doing this for far too long. During a previous relationship I had before Carly, I stayed with a girl for 6 months after realizing I didn't want to be with her because I knew we would be heart broken, and I swore to never do it again.

Meditation was becoming more than a place to clear my mind; it was as if that was becoming the reality, I wanted to experience more than this one. A sea to swim and fish for answers, making the right connections without trying to connect at all, letting my body relax and my mind open, give in, surrender, and accept all that has, is and will be.

My place where there was no judgment, no hate, no fingers pointed from any direction, just an encouraging place to be me and be myself. To be accepted for everything I was and everything I was not. I was hooked and reeled in through an ocean of completeness, which drenched my spirit with new awareness. I was starting to understand things that many people have studied for years, yet still struggled to grasp, but to me they just were floating into my way of thinking.

I was gaining the ability to see past the biological suit my consciousness was born into. Each time I went into that alone space, that little room where I could be away from everything and everyone, I would drift a little firmer into a trance that pulled, I would transcend and explore new lands.

I am a believer, and always have been. There is a lot more to this life than what meets the eye; there is something beyond what we can see. There is a deeper meaning to us, our purpose, our calling. Getting pulled towards someone, for a reason we cannot explain, and push away from someone too, not before what he or she said, or did not say, but because, we just do!

I am amazed by those that claim they can connect with the deceased, spirits from the other side.

I have witnessed it firsthand in spiritual church. I attended with my mum as she was seeking for answers, messages, and every time she did, my dad would always come through. He came with passion and sorrow. Asking for forgiveness for his actions and lack of. But mum never really forgave him, she is a very stubborn woman, as hard as nails. That's where I get my persistence from and toughness. She has been a role model for me and my sister, showing us how to stay strong no matter what life throws.

She buries her emotions deep, stuffs them down and blocks them out.

Something I have done too, maybe that is what I picked up from her, after all, I didn't have anyone else to admire and model when I was a young boy. She was a mother and a father, she wore both jackets, but still, there was a missing void.

And that is why I needed to go deeper into my meditation, to release the knots that were tying me down and stopping me from moving forward. I decided to join a class guided by an experienced instructor, before this my meditation was on my own for no longer than six minutes.

The session lasted for one-and-a-half hours and was conducted in a very warm and relaxing room filled with 20 other people all searching for peace, clarity, and prosperity. The difference about this session and my own practices was the self-imposed restriction. I was in a class, and removed from the right to get up and walk out. Sometimes we have the tendency to think that's enough for today, but when you have to stay until the bell sounded or you would disrupt everyone that was in deep focus, you stay to the end, and that is where the magic happens. But to stay in one still place for that length of time requires new levels discipline.

The whole experience felt magical to me. It felt as if I was everything and nothing all. I was disconnected from my body and my mind which was no longer filled with clutter and stress. It was clean, pure, and a space filled with positive emotions, love, and happiness. I felt blissful and free, filled with abundance and gratitude for being me.

To reach such a calm state, I followed my breath as it flowed in and out of me, letting go of any unwanted thoughts by just letting them slip away, this was all thoughts at that time.

I struggled to let go at first, but a voice inside made me feel safe enough to trust where I was going. I was no longer attached to any of the external beliefs that I thought made me.

I disconnected, yet felt connected. I continued to relax until there was nothing left besides my heartbeat, beating with the rest of the heart beats on this world, together as one.

I felt waves of energy, beats of love, amplified with such strength and power, fueled by the flow that I was receiving from deeper realms. I went into a vacuum of space; my thoughts something of the past, but I could feel them there through dancing colors of emotions.

We were brought back to our awareness by the instructor's soft, gentle tone, I was awake, able to think, but my body was not, I was conscious but had no feeling over my body, as if I was dead, trapped in the mind, unable to move! I was paralyzed, my body was out of reach, I started to panic a little, like anyone would waking up from the other side, not know what the hell had happened.

The struggle and mental fight must have jumpstarted my nervous system, as I could feel the blood circulating in my body. I could slightly move my fingers and toes, which was a relief from the trauma I was encountering. What happened next is something I will never forget; it was such a contrast.

As soon as my full awareness came back, I could feel the weight of my entire body, and it felt heavy. I could feel the pressure of the world push me down, dragging me to the ground, so I could surrender to her.

I could feel all the inflammation my body was holding, water retention, irritation in my joints, my stiffness, soreness. It was painful, and I didn't like it at all. Reality struck, the truth hurts, and this was home, no wonder I felt held back. The existing thoughts of the situation I was in started to build up around me, they were blocking my path, but not blocking me, I could see a clear direction to take to avoid any drama. I instantly felt the excitement to go back but not until I shifted the unnecessary weight, I was carrying that was dragging me down and pulling me back.

I was blown away by my experience. I was so excited to tell others too, but then I realized that the path to knowing is a lonely one and many won't understand.

This was the reason my father didn't open much about his understanding?

He told me so in his diary that he didn't care too much what people thought. That's why he didn't feel the need to tell too many about his new understanding, I know because that is how I felt, but I was loving the experience of the truth, knowing there is more beyond.

I continued my practice week after week, every Saturday evening. When most people would be getting ready to go out, I would be getting ready to go in!

Carly was a little bit confused how I was responding and the way I was starting to talk, sharing some of my new understanding of life and existence. It was a rapid shift in my awareness, which seemed like my personality. I was calm and caring but emotionless; I was becoming detached, like a robot.

My intuition was becoming stronger than ever, and so was I; even my dreams had more meaning. I was getting messages in my sleep that were so intense, I would wake and they would be on my mind for the rest of the day until I passed them onto whoever they were intended for. I know it sounds crazy, but its real. A few months before I would have thought the same, anyone talking the way I was certainly going crazy, but I wasn't. My mind was opening up, connecting to a portal, a pathway to other dimensions, and I was becoming awakened and I loved it; I wanted more.

When we have a taste of something so pure and rich that takes us to a place with only love and peace, it's hard to leave. We always want to go back, especially when our reality is shifting and the love we once felt is fading. We want to escape this disruption. We think about the next trip, like an addict.

During one of my sessions, I wanted to connect to whatever there was above. That was my highest intention, connecting with the divine source energy. I focused on this only and left everything else fade into the background.

I went into a trace again; I felt my body get lighter with each breath. I felt it descend and slowly drift from beneath me. The passing of ages between my soul and my body, time and fabric of space. My spirit rose higher and higher, I was floating on air, rising to the top of the room looking down at where my body laid. Detached physically and emotionally, although I felt engaged to it, connected somehow, as my consciousness was everywhere, I was everyone, wherever I choose to be, I was in control of my point of awareness.

It was a beautiful, spiritual experience that left me enlightened like no other.

As I slowly feathered down weightlessly and gently toward my blood pumping body, I could feel my heartbeat gradually getting louder with a vibrant thud and my vertical chambers opened and slammed shut to let rich blood circulate. Suddenly I was aware of the difference between my physical body and spiritual presence. I realized that I have the capability to do whatever I please with this gift of knowing. I am the conductor, and at my fingertips is the ability to create complete harmony between my spirit and body, synergistically working together. The Yin and Yang to life, bringing together two different forces to create an unlimited potential that could lead to extraordinary possibilities.

It then went completely dark and empty, which triggered my enthusiasm to seek the light. I could see a dim light in the distance on my mind. I felt the urgency to move my thought toward it; the light became my new intention.

As I got closer, it started forming a shape of an upside-down L shape, but at this point, the light was far brighter than it was before. I continued moving toward it, it became so bright, I felt the heat from it. It was beaming at me, with more strength than the sun. I continued and I could see that it was, a door that was almost shut, it had a little between the corner of the door and the doorframe. I knew that behind that door was all the power, energy, light, more ever seen. I had to open it, I was determined to, destined to, I needed to absorb this gift from above.

I reach for it, but I was just out of reach for some reason.

I tried and tried again, but I had no chance, it was right in front of me, but my journey stopped here. I started to get a little frustrated, and that's when I heard a voice deep from within me. It wasn't in my mind; it was in my emotions. It came as an intense gut-like feeling that said, "All awaits you, but not yet. You are not ready. Use what you have been given so far and help the people around you. They need that light, that uplift, then your time will come."

I relaxed and slowly started to feel myself drift away, being softly pulled toward my still body, like an astronaut in space drifting away from the gravity that once pulled him. But with a message that was delivered, and one I heard loud, bright, and clear. I traveled away and connected with my higher self. I was shown that there is more, way more, and that the very reason to receiving, is to pass on. So, and that not just I benefit but all that is around me do too.

A few days had passed, and I was thinking about the gift I was given. I didn't know what I needed, but I needed help from someone. But like anyone seeking help, I had to be prepared to relax and open up, which was all a little new to me.

I received a message from a friend who is also a healer.

She asked how I was and that it was time to meet up, she could feel it. We arranged to therapy session a few days later at her house.

I pulled up, went inside, sat on the table, started chatting. I always felt so comfortable with Dawn. Even though I have only spoken to her a few times, I had heard so much about her beforehand that I felt instantly connected with her.

Dawn had helped me a few weeks back in our first session. She has a psychic ability to receive message and the emotional intelligence to deliver in the way that's easiest to digest and absorb.

So I begin, take off my shoes, lay on the sofa, and get into a comfortable position. I closed my eyes, relaxed my body, calmed my heart, and began go into myself. After a few, short, visual exercises to relax my senses, I was zoning in as I was zoning out.

Dawn guided me into my imagination. I was walking down a long, wet, dirty old staircase that led to a door with a big, rusty, round doorknob. It was the biggest handle I had ever seen. So big, it needed two hands to try opening.

I placed my hands on it, but it was apparent that I had a problem letting go and trusting what was ahead. I was holding back from exploring the layers of my existence that define my character, the infrastructure that makes me the person I am today, the memories I have locked in tightly, hidden away, chosen to forget.

But Dawn's soft voice was there with me, and she made me feel safe, relaxed, and reassured. She kept reminding me that this was a choice, I wasn't being forced to go inside. I could come away anytime I wanted. I grasped the handle with both hands, turned it anti-clockwise which was really tough to do, because I was holding back from using all my might. I heard a voice from within whisper, "Go on, you can" so I proceeded and turned the doorknob open, which felt like turning the wheel on a yacht. The door slowly opened and my throat went instantly dry and tight. It opened into a place in the sky overlooking so much free land, miles of greenery that was nourished with life. I stood at the edge, gazing at the earthly world before me. I couldn't believe this was what I feared, this was behind the door, what I was putting off for so long.

I took a moment to appreciate where I was, from where I had been. I stared upon acres of endless valleys filled with life that roamed peacefully. There were rivers flowing fresh water, birds tweeting. If there was a place such as heaven, I imagined it would be like this. It was perfect, clean, fresh, and naturally organic. I felt so present in the moment, far beyond the meditation adventures I had been on. Dawn's gentle voice was with me, guiding me down from the height of the doorway that seemed to just be in mid-air, like an opening to a different reality. I walked across the natural land toward the river and glanced down to my feet. I noticed I was wearing light-brown sandals and had a white gown wrapped around my body. I felt naked underneath, stripped, but it didn't concern me, I felt clean. I was comfortable, comfortable with being me.

I passed a few deer and many other friendly animals, the were not alarmed, they were relaxed. I noticed three men by the river, squatted down, drinking. They looked very different to me and what I was used to seeing. They didn't have clothes on. Their hair was long, the beards were too. I could also sense a little fear, fear from the unknown, because I knew they had never seen someone like me before, but I didn't feel judged or threatened, I felt like I was here to help.

In my peripheral vision sported something that soon changed the tranquility I was feeling. I noticed a castle, which had a completely different feel surrounding it. I felt my body instantly go cold; it sent a shiver down my spine. I sensed it was somewhere I wanted to avoid but felt like I shouldn't. It changed my entire experience. I felt the fear soak me, like the river I was now standing in. I wanted to turn around, but my feet felt heavy. I looked down at the water and I saw the fear in my eyes. I turned to walk away and I saw the same look in the men's eyes that were still staring at me.

They were fearful of the unknown just like me, but I sensed they had hope, hope that I would lead the way. I took a deep breath in and started walking toward the dull, grey castle.

As I got closer, I recognized it. It was the very one I went to school in many years ago, Cyfarthfa Castle in Merthyr Tydfil, but now it looked different. It looked deserted and abandoned. It was covered in thick, wet moss, the fountains that once ran with clean water had long been shut off. The big lake that was in front of the castle was now just a dry, dusty, and an old bed of weeds. The sky above was miserable, filled with violent clouds which made it far from inviting.

I walked over, through the muddle garden, battling my nerves as I made my way through the path toward my fate, shivers running through my body as I once again was about to face my fears. By this time, there was a gathering of people, they all came to watch me confront my fear and take on the frightening castle.

I got to the front door, and I was met again by another doorknob. I turned it and I walked inside my castle. The door slammed behind me, sending echoes down the hallway. What was bizarre about the inside was it was a lot different to the castle I went to school in, plus it was completely empty.

There was no dust or dirt, no sound or movement, no fear or negativity; there was nothing or anybody. I walked around and I saw a bendy staircase that was heading to the rooftop, which seemed a long way up. Floor after floor for as far as I could see, but I wanted to climb. I put my hand on the rail, looked up to what looked like a never-ending staircase, and I took on the challenge.

I focused only on one step at a time, didn't stop, or look up, just kept going endlessly until I finally put my foot on the top step. I was met by yet another door with another handle on it. I opened it, this time with no hesitation. The stairway went on and continued outside, above the castle, leading up to a doorway high in the sky like the one I had come from.

I was reminded by the doorway in my meditation session that I was trying to reach for but couldn't, this gave me a second boost, because I felt like now was the time.

The higher I climbed, the more I felt my spirit was rising, like it did when I was leaving my body. My confidence had grown. I felt so strong, powerful, and clear about my intentions.

I looked down to the many now-shocked faces. Their eyes were wide open too, I felt connected to each one's soul, like I was inserting a life lesson for them to experience. I could hear them whisper to each other, but continue make out the words, although the meaning was clear, they were proud that I was overcoming something no one has ever attempted but so many have thought about doing, held back by their fears.

This made me more determined, desirous, and dedicated to get to the top and open that final door. It was no longer about me. It was about them, leading the way, leading by example.

I took the last step again, and before me stood a pure white door that seemed to be positioned perfectly in glooming sky with a breathtaking panoramic background hung like a picture, polished and clean, like a heavenly gate.

I smiled as I opened the door to let the glory that was concealed hit me and flood me with the bright light I felt, like my supernova.

I expressed to Dawn what I could feel and she asked where I wanted to go now. I replied, "Back down, to help those below, the ones in darkness, in pain, the ones that need to realize the truth."

She asked me, "What truth?"

"That on the other side of fear is everything you ever dreamt of and more; it's pure bliss," that is the message I must give, I said.

I floated back down and I was once again standing outside the castle I went to school in, but the set had changed, the people around me were different. They were kids, kids I knew, kids I went to school with. Now the castle was exactly as I remembered it before. That is because it was not my imagination, I was in a deep memory.

Revisiting, reliving, a memory I remember well but didn't think it had much significance to my future, but obviously it did.

The diary

A dream

A white light filled with the soft bewilderment.

Motion slowed down

Angels glided gently down

And the beginning of perfection had begun.

There was no pain.

The white light was not the effects of nuclear harness ray, it was the will of God.

Everybody and everything rejoiced.

Chapter 10
What I Was Seeking Was Seeking Me

It was a warm summer afternoon. It was a regular day at school, nothing different or unique, but what was certainly different was how I felt. I don't know why but I felt a little lost, as if I didn't know if I liked the boy I was becoming.

I lost my uncle not so long ago along with my cousin in a devastating car crash which left so much collateral damage. I had always hung out with older boys; it's just how it was. We would learn from those above us, but what we didn't realize is what we were being taught was wrong.

They would steal, fight in gangs, and get in trouble. I guess it was because we all back then felt we had something to prove and we all carried a bit of a chip on our shoulders. The older boys would make us younger boys fight for their amusement. They would psych us up until we were like little aggressive Pitbull terriers preparing to charge at our victims, then throw us at each other in the ring they created around us, and bet who would win. We were trying to win their respect, trying to fit in, feel big, as big as they seemed.

I was playing football in the school grounds, the ball got kicked over the fence, so I ran to get it and the boy in front of me slammed the gate against my hand. I am not sure if he meant to do it or was it an accident, but either way I was furious, he could see that too, so he ran. I ran after him, but as he was a good foot taller than me, he was pretty fast, a little faster than me. One thing I always had, even back then, was the ability to not give up, so I kept running, chasing him around the castle, which sparked so much excitement to the other kids as they were running too. After some time, he slowed down to catch his breather, I caught him, and all the other kids caught up to catch the action.

"Fight," they chanted. "Hit him," they yelled. I clenched my fist and swung my arm back to gain the momentum so I could plummet a punch into his face and teach him a lesson. He looked petrified, terrified. He was crying for mercy, begging me to not hit him. But I had too, I couldn't stop now, not with every kid in the school behind me, egging me on to punch him. The pressure was too much, like it was when I was six years old, when I cried because everyone around me wanted me to cry at my father's funeral. I closed my eyes and drove my dense fist into his sad face. I instantly felt terrible, I didn't want to hit him; he didn't deserve it. But there was a certain level of expectation that was demanded of me; I felt I had to prove myself as worthy of acceptance.

That is when Dawn's voice came in. She asked me to go back to just before I hit him and instead of doing what I thought everyone wanted me to, do what I wanted to do. So, I did.

I dropped my hand down, looked at him in his eyes, and said, "I was sorry." I then turned to all the others that wanted me to punch him and told them that it's not the right thing to do. Their faces dropped with disappointment, faces, I really let them down, the respect I had was gone, I was a disappointment.

Dawn suggested I imagined I had returned to school the following day and I was walking into the castle, into the long corridor that led to my classroom.

I could see all the same disappointed faces looking at me, all muttering things about me, how they thought I was different, how they thought I wasn't a tough guy, how I let them down. I felt so embarrassed as I walked through the lines that gathered on both sides, it was the walk of shame leading to death row, as my life felt like it could not come back after such social embarrassment. I felt judged, and a little used, frustrated, angry and confused all in one mush of thought.

Dawn asked me to focus on people that loved me for who I was, not what I did, and to imagine them at the end of the corridor waiting for me to get to them.

There are two people that have always been there for me, my mother and my sister, so I visualized them standing right at the end, which gave me hope. I could see them smiling, calling me with open arms, I had faith that all would be ok when I got to them, which motivated me to keep going and block out the noise from others. Everything else was just background noise at this point. I was so connected to the love they were sending me, and I felt secure.

I reached the end, where they were waiting, put my arms around them and hugged them. They looked at me and told me they love me for who I am, not for what I have done, or will do. They said they were so proud of me being so brave to do what I wanted, and they thanked me for giving them the encouragement to do the same.

Dawn told me to keep that feeling with me as I turned and walked back through the crowd of whispers. I could hear them talking about me again. I listened in curious to what they had to say. They were saying how proud they were too, and that I was different from the rest, different to what they thought I was, but different in the way you only wish to be.

It was a completely different feeling, a different experience of the truth, it was all a matter of perception, once I changed my emotional state, my world changed.

Boom, like a lightning bolt it hit me, the realization, I'd been living in a lie since I was 6 years old. Trapped into a way of thinking, changing my behaviors to become what I thought others wanted me to be. Ignoring what I really wanted to be, how I wanted to respond to situations which involved the emotion of someone else. To be concerned about what they would think, worries about what they say, how they would make me look, and how I would make them feel. But the truth is it was all in my head, and the only person my actions were affecting was me. I realized that other people are so concerned with their reality, dealing with the operation of their own mind, they did not care too much about me. And if they did try to change me just to suit their needs, then they obviously did not care about me, so why would I care about them.

I could see countless similar situations in my life where I was a seeking the approval of others.

I had a breakthrough, a new discovery about myself and the understanding of the world I was in, I was the artist painting my way, bringing any ideal to reality.

By stumbling across this knot that was hidden in my memory, I untangled so many more that were limiting my potential. I was free, relaxed, able to make sharper decisions that were aligned with what I wanted, and God only knows I want to be the best I can be.

I drifted back into my senses, complete with gifted awareness which was more than what I left with on this trip down memory lane.

I opened my eyes, and for the first time in a long time I could see clearer, I whipped the tears from my face, got up, and smiled.

Dawn gave me some post-therapy guidance to follow, because the time after such deep regressions and realizations, is where it can make or break you.

It is important to understand what you experienced to avoid falling into a state of confusion, which is very common after one unravels the threads that are holding their life as they know it together. Especially when one realization that they are where they are in life because of them and no one else. The choices they made, and the opportunities they missed because they were too ignorant to see.

She told me to spend some time on my own, no music, no phone calls, no influence, just me and my thoughts. But I could not stop thinking about my dad, the decisions he made, and the regret he was living with. I felt sad thinking, if only he was able to receive this type of help, maybe his story, the battle he was in would have been completely different. He would have discovered what I did, that it was all in his head, and got control of it.

Then he would be here today, telling his story himself with his words, instead of a student of his pen.

A few days later I started to notice the change everywhere. I was able to see the separation from my desire and what was desired of me. I was aware that it was my mindset whilst in the environment I was in, that was molding my character.

Entertaining the audience, I was in front of just to spray some memorable moments of joy.

But now I had no attachment at all, I could just be me.

I could see that many of the issues and problems other people have in their lives, this was from a non-judgement position, it was from an observant one. I had been observing myself, which taught me more about others.

Most of the problems we have are internal, rooted within our minds. We are what we choose to be, and we can choose to be whatever we want. We are in control, in control of our feelings, in control of our response to other people.

'If you want to change the world, start with yourself.' By Mahatma Gandhi.
This is one of my favorite quotes. This is another, 'If you change the way you look at the things, the things you look at change,' by Wayne Dyer.

I have read these so many times, repeated them so many more, but never really understood the true meaning until that day.

The weight of the world had lifted off my beaten down shoulders, free from all the worry that was holding me back. I was confident I would not absorb any painful animation that was fired towards me, aimed by anyone trying to hurt. I would shield myself, reflect it and in return send out my love and blessing to them. Hoping that my intention is to better the world I am in, which is their world too.

My relationship was being tested, and that brought more arrows my way, but I was in a calm state of mind, and so it has a chance to evolve. The knowing that it was meant to be like this for us both, we would get through.

We had been through worse, this was another opportunity to learn from, adapt to, and emerge into the next gifted challenge.

I had so much more yet to understand and realize, which left me in much confusion, I was questioning everything, and I liked it, as it led to more truths. There were more discoveries out there, in there. I believed what was coming, was already here, as I could feel it nearby. I knew that everything would come together, and I would start putting all pieces of the puzzle together.

I knew that there was far more availability than I could ever begin to imagine, and that one life would ever be enough to obtain all this understanding, which got me excited because I knew I would be on a quest until the day I died.

I was trusting in my intuition, my gut feeling. I knew they were messages from my higher self-guiding me in the right direction. It had been sending signals, suggesting we needed time apart. We were not on the right path to our potential future. And that was not part of the cosmic plan. We needed to find our own way first; we needed to find ourselves. It became too strong, I couldn't ignore. I tried but before, before I knew less. There was no way I could bury it, it would eat at me until I dug it back up, and by that time it would burst out. It was causing so much eruption in me, so I use my discipline to my advantage as a sedative. I shut down all feelings, stopped the response to anything. I was numb, emotionless, unhuman, like a robot, a machine without a connection to anyone else, just me. I was strolling through each day, cold and lifeless it seemed. But the real battle was going on within, between my mind and heart. I wanted to be with Carly, we were meant for greatness; I knew it, I felt it, I saw it, it was a vision I had but not like this, we were not ready. We were in each other's way, holding each other back.

My new attitude toward life was hard for her to grasp. Everyone was more confused; Carly was more than me. She would be always upset, crying most night, asking me questions too difficult to answer without upsetting her; there was more suffering and heartache.

It was either I did not feel the same way as she did or that I was just tolerating it better, or maybe I had convinced myself that I do not feel pain with the understanding that pain is in the mind, and everything that goes on in the mind is an illusion. I was at the point where I didn't feel at all, well, apart from her slipping away, or me letting her go, that depends on how you look at it. I would hold her hands every night, look her in the eye, and tell her everything was going to be okay; everything will work out for the better, I promised! And I never break a promise, I knew it would be, I knew we would be happier, my intuition told me.

I had a responsibility to help her, not just because she was my wife but I knew I had a calling. The message I received that told me to help others discover what I had so they could also see the truth, the truth I was once blinded to. That is why I was trusting everything, going along with the experience, and accepting my fate.

We have to, trust the process with the faith to continue, knowing it will be impactful on this life, or the next, which is any future moment, because that moment is the creation of a new life.

They say you should never make promises you can't keep, which I agree. I knew; I was certain. I could see it like a movie playing over in my mind, like it had already been lived, a premonition. I saw myself; I was immensely powerful, a well-respected figure with lots of authority but also so much love. I would go on to help thousands of people globally, sharing my word of wisdom on stages so many dying inside people, with endless hope of a brighter day.

I saw Carly too; she was a woman of power and respect also. Helping so many women get through their struggles, similar to what she has gone through.

She was loved from her authenticity, and compassion for others.

We were smartly dressed, proud, confident, and happy for each other. Best friends, supporting one another to succeed. We didn't need anyone or anything to make us feel love, because we loved ourselves, and the world we were in.

What I did not know is, if we would be together as a couple, I couldn't see that deep, which I know is for a reason, like everything else.

I expressed to her too what I saw, which caused a lot of confusion and suffering. But I had to be honest, and I was not affected like I used to be about other people's reactions.

I am an extrovert, an open book, with so much life in me, the energy oozes out. I never sugarcoat my words too; I tell it as it is. It's part of my job and I get paid for my honest feedback, even if it is not always welcomed.

During one of meditation sessions, I went in deep, like I always did, I was on a quest to find out what I really wanted, my highest intention and truest potential.

I wanted to discover what was seeping the life out of my relationship so I could find the cracks and fill them.

I had so many questions I never discussed, but I knew I would find answers in my happy place, inside me. I wanted to understand the reason why we were no longer compatible, what we both really wanted, which was not giving each other. Why there was emptier space between us, as we pushed each other further away.

I thought of all the past pleasurable experiences which we had together and how she helped me through tough days, days that would have been unpleasant if she weren't there. How she was there when I was overcoming my fears, when I was expanding my mind, exploring my spirituality. How she was with me through all my adventures and at my awaking on new consciousness. How she was there even when she was not. How I had missed the energy she once brought.

It started to become clearer. It was clear and I didn't even see it before, but like many of my newfound understanding, it was all starting to make sense.

I wanted someone to see me for who I really was, that was my intention. Someone that was non-judgmental and accepted me. Someone that let me be me, that connected with me on a level that is hard to explain in words.

I opened my eyes and I knew this would be life-changing. I didn't know what it would lead to, but I knew there was a reason for everything and there was another for this.

I got home. I walked in the bedroom where she was sitting drying her hair. She looked so fresh and clean but empty inside.

I told her about my meditation session. As I did, I started to cry, with mixed emotions, passion, and sorrow.

The flood came, and would not stop, the path to knowing was a lonely one, that I always knew, but now I was taken it, and deciding to take it too.

Everything that past was to get to this point, and what got me here was not what would get me there.

I needed to be on my own, I wanted to be on my own, my life depended on it and my life was the most important, as it was the only life I truly knew.

I knew some would say it was a selfish act but every action is, as to act without the mind of the self would mean to be selfless, and to be selfless is death.

And death, although not understood, is the one encounter we all experience in this life, whether we want to, or not, whether we take ourselves there early, or let nature play its part through the hands of time.

The opposite for living a lie, is dying for truth. And during my experience locked away from all my senses, from all my thoughts and feeling, I was shown both sides of the coin, I was introduced to an idea, that one cannot simply exists without the other.

I knew I needed time on my own, time apart from everyone. I needed to work on me, find myself, free from all the confusion, the clutter, and chronic stress.

I realized that what I had been seeking all this time was also seeking me; and that was me. All the answers are within the center of my everything, and I was the center of everything.

It was I that was controlling all around, the good, the bad, the love, the hate, the pleasure, the pain, my life, and my death. All that was seen, heard, felt, experienced, could not exist without the opposite to that, nor could the closing of a book, that was never opened. It's a flip of a coin, one that will fall in a position you need, which would depend on the hand that threw it, on that environment it was released into, and the condition of the ground it fell on to.

But it is never a gamble, good luck or bad, it is what it is and what it is, is what it is destined to!

The diary

Lord, lead me to soften my heart.

I don't wish to be a hardhearted man. Lord, lead me to the softness there in and I know you can.

I don't want to judge others and I hope they don't judge me, but I know they do and it makes me blue, yet to this I agree.

That I'll try my best, God, in future I truly will, and I'll paint something wonderful because it is your will.

Thy will be done.

Chapter 11
The Break

I could feel it again, that feeling you get when you know the outcome of what is to come even before it does, and you are just waiting to see or hear it. I believe Carly had the same feelings as me, but she was never aware, so she was never able to understand, and expressed to me.

I parked my car outside our home and I knew she wasn't there, she was gone. I felt it, she was missing, and had been for some time. I wasn't sure if it was what I actually wanted or not, but I wasn't happy, that's for sure, I was on my way down.

I walked in the apartment we lived in for just over a year, but it no longer felt like my home. It was filled with thoughts of passed arguments, cold memory that seemed to trigger the feeling of loneliness. I sat down on the sofa, closed my eyes and removed my thoughts from the depressed state I was in. I just let my mind wander down memory lane. It was not long before I revisited many happy memories, we both had together. We were so joyful and in love, but they started to fade, like they were tough to hold on too, they were distant memories. This created a feeling of anxiety as it felt like they could be the last time happy memories we created together. Which was a tough pill to swallow, even though I thought I could take anything!

I felt a numbness in my chest as it got so tight, it became hard to breathe, like my oxygen was being cut off and I started to panic. There was a twisting knot in my stomach, like someone was rinsing out a soaked towel in there, draining all the wetness, flooding my being, this was followed with intense contractions, as if I was giving birth, by letting go of a life that was part of me.

My eyes started building up which led to tears streaming out of them, I cried like I had never cried before. I was crying my heart out, literally! I felt as though someone was ripping my heart out of the insertions, breaking it in two and draining the love that once filled it, the love that bound two together.

I could not keep still, it was agonizing, like nothing I ever felt in my life. I fell to my knees, and started cradling myself on the ground. I was at the point of breaking, and I realized I needed to be break, I knew I had to go through it, the process of acceptance and letting go.

I cried out loud, I felt sorry for myself. The emotional pain was thought new meaning to the word POWER, it was above me, beyond me, and I have taken my body to some extremes, but this was from somewhere emotional energy we simply could not generate.

I looked at myself in the mirror through my bloodshot eyes and asked, "Why me? Why me? Why are we breaking up when she is my everything? Why must we go through this even if I don't want to, I don't understand, why?"

This went on for some time, repeating the same word, experiencing the same pain and feeling the same hurt. I was confused, overwhelmed, begging for my savior. The headache I had from mind working like a steam train of the track I was once on, felt my head feeling like it was wedged in a clamping device.

Then it went silent, nothing but stillness, my heart slowed down as if it was no longer at beat, my space become as if I was underwater, pause in a moment of calmness, as my world came to a rest. A gentle voice came as a thought, but one that I did not think of. *Christian. This will only make you stronger. It will make you both stronger. You must trust the process; you must have faith.*

I wiped my face dry, as the tears had stopped. My breathing was in control, I felt protected, surrounded by unconditional love. I was in the presence of another, which I have always been. He is always there for me, listening to my cries, picking me up when I am down, and comforting me when I am in pain, I just never had the pleasure of meeting him before this day. I knew there is eternal love for me, and I had made a connection to receive.

I needed to experience this level of pain and heartache, this kind of trauma, I needed to hurt from the death, the death within me, the death of part of me.

I had lost someone close, closer that all the people I have lost before, but none of them ripped my heart out, nor did I rip my heart out for any of them. But for us both I did, because that is how much I cared, how much I wanted us both to be free, broken and in a place to rebuild.

I needed to feel it, to understand what other's experience, the suffering and the grief over; I needed to feel human, instead of a machine.

It was the time, my time, time to focus on the bigger picture behind all this painting of life's colorful emotions. I knew that everything is positioned perfectly in place at precisely the right time in order to grow. I had a lot of growing to do, which meant everything was going to get only better, even if it brings days that feel worst.

I accepted my chosen path was a lonely one, and I pondered if that was what was meant for me, that I am meant to be on my own, alone, but connected to source for the better of all.

I knew success would come at a cost to pay, everything in life has a tax, even the life you live. I knew that the art of creating opportunities to better other people's life, although it would better mine, it would require the sacrifice of it. I was told to aim for the top because the bottom is crowded. The top has more room, yet there are fewer people up there to share it with. But I knew I didn't have to take this path, I wasn't held at gun point, I was just shown the gate to it, and I walked through. But you can never go back, you can stand still where you are, and not take another step forward, that is a choice, but once you know, you know, it stays within.

Carly came home later that night. She had spent several hours chatting with the owner of the salon she works at. They had become good friends, they got on well and Helen sort of a mentor to her, a great mentor too. She was a little older, maybe wiser, and understood her well enough for her advice to be welcomed. Carly told me that she suggested it would be best for her to move out for a short while, in that time, we could have some space and time apart. Carly told me that she already decided it was for the best, and that she had already booked an apartment close to her work for the next five days, after this she would be looking to extend or find somewhere new for some more time apart.

I told her I think it would be a good idea too, and I would support her decision.

She collected her things, packed them in a suitcase, and said goodbye. The night went fast, as it was already late. I knew she was gone before she said she was, the arch was already out in the sea at float, ready to ride whatever waves will come.

The next morning came, I woke up was fully focused, driven by my north star. The life quest of becoming the best I can be. Climbing that peak, reaching my truest potential, letting the past pass, and disconnecting with anyone that was not aligned with my vision.

I was fixated on an idea, a way of thinking. There was no backing down. Although I was not willing to step on anyone to get there, as that simply was not me, but I made a decision to cut ties with anyone that tries to stop me, push me back, or pull me down. No way, if they were in my way, there was only one place they were going, and that was out of it.

I knew I would not need to use any physical force at this point, I would be protected by my guides, as I took the route to a road that was meant for me, constructed by a higher force, driven by a purpose bigger than me.

I was in service to help all. It would flow to me naturally if I stayed on this track. To help the masses, impact so many, grow my brand, get the recognition I will need. Build the relationships and the network that will help me be seen from afar, with the desire to inspire, leading by an example, and follow our preordained path.

I was committed to make the sacrifice on any relationship that tries to toy with my emotions, and deviated my direction, as for me to fly a straight arrow, I need my eyes focused on the bull, and not aroused by the red flags.

I may be a spiritual being, but I am living it through a physical body, that has all the emotions we are blessed to use, and all the ones we pray we don't have to.

Throughout my life I have had to accept the death of many loved ones, it was something I have always been able to get over kind of fast, move on, and get on with it.

This one would be no different, apart from the fact I had obtained more experience, I was equipped to do again, but even better.

This was a special for sure, and I believe the codes ran deeper than the rest, but never the less, the sun is up, and I had woken!

It rose with the energy that would life the fields it connected to, it had rising to over its light, and bring new opportunities for a brighter future tomorrow, and so was I.

I was alert, with passion driven ideas, and gift of knowing on how to spark their life, and nurture their development.

I tackled the days that would follow with such focus, using my intuition like the horns on a bull, charging one way, and that was forward. I was building a future, working on improving my strengths and weaknesses. I was running a business, looking after my clients, documenting loads of content for an app I was about to launch, making new connections, creating speaking opportunities. I was turning up, on time, with no second guessing about my decisions, getting it done. I knew I need to balance my energies, now aware of both sides of the coin, so I was meditating a lot more too. Calming the mind, relaxing the body, then pushing even further, but not harder, effortlessly flowing,

I was seeking light in all lighter, as the more that awaits, and building a stronger relationship with another, I was starting to love being with me. Meditation was another therapy, a coping mechanism with the stresses of life, as well as my training, but what was very peculiar, although they were polar opposites, one could not function well, without the other. I was transferring the push that weight training had taught me, into pushing for heights in vibration and spiritual contact with the Devine, as well as the discipline bodybuilding taught me. I was also transferring the idea I learnt through mediation of non-attachment, and the benefit of focused breathing to my bodybuilding workouts. I never thought they would accommodate each other, as they were two opposites, but my new discovery was that opposites do not work well together, but they are the halve that make the whole.

When I was training, I mastered how to silence my thoughts, slow down my heartbeat, which allowed me to peak perform and recover so much faster, it was my new playground to test my new findings from my meditation.

There were opening channels that I didn't know existed, which allowed me to see different ways to achieve success. And it was all just a matter of mindset, like everything else.

I was married before I met Carly, to a mindset. A way of thinking, one that led me to success, which I have unconditional love for. But because I was so ignorant to see any other way, or maybe I had my guard up so high protecting my ego, I was blinded to the truth of their existence. Either way, I have unconditional love for everything that has been before me, for that made me.

I was a young boy, surrounded by a lot of negative energy. I found myself in situations that took me out of character, acting a way I didn't want to, leading a life I thought I would regret. I was frustrated, angry, aggressive, and violent. I was a confused adolescent trying to find my way.

The day I decided to change the way I looked because I was tired of how it made me feel changed my life forever. It took me from the street and introduced me to the love of my life, the gymnasium.

I fell in love with the weights. Aw you should have seen my face whenever I could escape and lift. We got engaged, it was a relationship that I knew, and still do, will last forever, I can feel it bedded deep into my roots of existence.

I used all the negative emotion to push my body so hard, to its limits. I would take all that express myself, releasing all the anger. I was there every day; I had a lot of anger to release.

It was incredibly helpful, it showed me another way to act out, without hurting others. It is what got me away from the crowd I was in, and God only knows where I would be now, if it weren't for the gym.

I married the idea that negativity was a great tool that would lead to so much positivity. Even when I was no longer in that negative situation, I would create one in my mind, I would internally live through some terrible thoughts, which would start a fire in my head, then a fire in my heart, and provide a war of fire so I use to push heavy weights as many times could and feel the burn, like a blowtorch burning my muscles to a crisp.

In return, I also build a lot more muscle. I would receive more attention, which created more opportunity, and I would become more influential and fitness leader in the industry. I gained sponsorship from supplement companies, clothing companies, food-prep companies. I was getting free gym membership at some local gyms. I was essentially getting all the things I needed for to help me push even harder, and grow even more muscle and provide me with even more. I went on to win bodybuilding championships, placing in the top 5 at the British finals for 6 years in a row; 5th, 4th, 3rd, 2nd, 2nd again, every place but first.

I went on the represent the U.K. at the World Championships, 5th in the Mr. Universe. I built a solid foundation for a growing business from what bodybuilding taught me, but also from what can be achieved by using the negative energy and fueling a positive movement.

It led to so much positivity on the outside, but I was feeling a little run down on the inside before I found meditation.

I was tired, it was exhausting, I was abusing myself without even knowing it, not physically, but mentally and emotionally.

I would psych myself up before the workout, thinking of people that had nothing nice to say about me, thinking more about the people that had bad things to say. You will never make it, you are nothing, you have nothing to give, there is no point even trying. Half of the thoughts I would think of I was creating on the spot, anything to make me furious, to boil my blood.

Repeating the negative things people said to me growing up, like I was, I was weak, stupid, fat, ugly. It would channel the urgency to prove them wrong.

It was a nightmare in my mind, created by me, and I was meant to love me right, then why you make ask, and the answer is, I never thought of how it could affect me. One of the reasons why people stay in an abusive relationship for too long, they are simply not aware of the damage it is doing.

Filling my mind with all these thoughts was reprogramming me to think these things and feel a way about myself, and I did it daily, over and over again, for many years.

The meditation allowed me to see that I could achieve so much more from being in a calmer state and only focus on one thing. Not the past, not the future, but that current moment. Focus on my breath and my highest intentions. By zoning in, I was able to zone out. I continued my practices during my workouts too as an experiment. As a result, I was able to feel everything; how much my body was functioning and how my mind was in control, not my body. I was able to enjoy the present and be completely absorbed in it. My lifts went up; I performed for longer; I was recovering better; my nervous system didn't seem as fatigued. But the most attractive thing about dating this new mindset was that I saw my body change before me. I got leaner faster, tighter, bigger, harder, and stronger. So, I was finally able to breakup, divorce one way of thinking and marry another, one that didn't make me feel bad about being myself, a mindset that didn't drag me down by dragging up the past. It didn't leave me feeling frustrated, exhausted, or beaten up. I accepted me for who I was, and I married an idea that was aligned with how I was thinking in the doing of the now.

I guess what I needed to learn and understand, what I needed to see, was that this mindset was causing more harm than good. It was destructive with the intention of being constructive. It was holding me back to what I could become. It was not aligned with my thoughts anymore. It no longer served purpose. It helped me get to the point of where I was, but it was no longer needed for where I was going.

Maybe detaching away from this relationship was allowing me to view my marriage as a similar thing but in a different sense. As I was happier than I had been for a long time since spending more time alone, I was finding me. I was understanding more about life and my gifts, the opportunities that were opening for me, the people that were coming into my life, people that had been there before. Maybe all the signs were there long before I finally saw them or chose to take notice.

I hadn't spoken to Carly for a while as she blocked my number. She most likely wanted to focus on herself too, which I understood and gave her space. After all, she did move out and I had no idea where she was. I was still living in the same apartment, always home at night, always available at the other side of the phone if she needed me or wanted me. I thought, *I am not hard to find.* The problem was that people expected me to chase her and that I'd be falling apart. Assuming I was depressed, and miserable, but that was not the way I chose to be. I was moving forward; nothing was stopping me. I didn't see any of this as a roadblock.

I was starting to feel very alone, except for my dad. He was near more than ever. Every time I came home, I felt his presence. He was there, guiding me from above, helping me get over my struggles, the struggles he never did get over. He was giving me strength from his whispers, the nudges in the right direction, and the confidence to keep going. My life was not ending, it was beginning.

One evening, I had a message from him. It came as a thought, how they always did. He told me to reach out to my mum and tell her that he was sorry, that he never meant to hurt her, that he will always be there for her. He told me she deserves the best. The best is yet to come, and he is sorry.

When I opened my eyes, I could see it so clearly. The reason he had never left was deeper than just to guide me. That was part of his role. He was living through me, helping me move forward in life, helping me make the right choices, proving to all that, it doesn't have to end that way. We can get over struggles and pain! We can turn our life around for the better.

He has been begging for forgiveness even before he left his body. He was not all bad in his doing, he created me, and he has guided me to the man I am today and the man I will become. He is living a life he never did, with me, through me. With my wisdom and spiritual connection, my relationship with him, we can create a better life for my mum, remove all the dirt that has been built over the pain and shine our loving light on it. Show her how special she is to us.

After some time apart, Carly came back home, but it was not for long. She tried, I tried, we tried, but it was just hopeless. The reality was that we were not used to be and we were far from where we were meant to be. She had been really struggling to deal with the time apart. The issue was that she wanted more than what I was giving and what I was willing to give.

She wanted more of my affection, which she deserved. But I was sticking to my guns even if it did not quite make sense to me at that time. I had faith, belief and I knew it was somehow that we needed desperately.

She was depressed, something she had felt for a while but pushed it down deep and buried it. She told me it started after her mum died, but she ignored it, or maybe didn't even. She was not aware how pushing your feeling down can lead to and how they can build up to the point you cannot stop from rising to the surface.

With everything we were going through and the fact she had a scare at the doctors around the same time, it seemed too much for her. She obviously felt alone too, we had never been apart, despite the fact she was thousands of miles away from her family. She felt disconnected from her husband, and was missing her mum for a hug.

I felt her pain, but I did not carry it with guilt, I did not feel responsible. I would have before, but after my therapy I was not letting what I thought other people wanted me to be, stop me from being the person I wanted to be.

We are all on our own journey. It's nobody's fault. It is up to us to fix any problems we find ourselves in. I will always love her, support her, and help her get through anything. She is still my best friend. It's just I didn't feel that way for her anymore. To be honest, I didn't feel much at all. I had shut down that part of me, stopped me feeling for others and was starting to feel for me only, as I was aware to love others you have to love yourself, my love was still growing. But I was in such a state of confusion, I would be very defensive with my emotions and switched them off. I became less interested in anything other than me, which seemed to allow me to become more aware with my soul's purpose and bring light to things I was too ignorant to see. It is not like I hated people, but I was working towards my goal, building internal bridges, then I could let others in to share them.

Many friends and family thought I had lost my mind, which, on times, I questioned it too. I felt so different, so much new information to absorb and try to make sense of.

I remember when I was just a kid and my friends used to say how my father was crazy, how he lost his mind and was weird, a loon. At the time, I thought it was just name-calling, but obviously that was the talk of the town back then. Him, similar to how it was for me.

After reading his diary, I found myself questioning the same, had he lost his mind? But from being on the receiving end of such judgment with many fingers pointed towards me, I can relate to how it can feel. Having people that know you well, that you have love and respect, disrespect you and your beliefs. Suggesting that you have lost your marbles. And that you need to see a shrink, take some medication and laugh at you sat with your legs crossed and eyes closed in meditation. There must be something wrong with him, he thinks he's Jesus Christ, not Christian.

It seemed that every time I spoke my mind, shared my thoughts, was honest about our true feelings, I felt regret for doing so. It left me a little more embarrassed and ashamed, as well as confusion, which is not the reason one choses to share, nor is it encouraging to.

It's the same reason many people don't open up and talk; the reason why my father didn't! The reason many bury their true desires with them in the grave they lay to rest. But my father was smart enough to write them in a diary, one that, when the time was right, I would read. A time when I needed his guidance to help me get through the same struggles he faced. He created a story that could save my life, and one that took his. So, his someone else could prepare for the storm that is coming, and make it through to the land of new opportunities. That was his sacrifice, but one that will not die with him, it will live on, because my sacrifice is to spend the time needed, to share my vulnerabilities, and help others prepare.

Even Carly was talking about her feelings a lot more and opening up, she could see how helpful it was becoming for me. She even decided to go to see a psychiatrist which I thought was a great idea. I asked if she wanted me to come, but she wanted to go on her own. She needed to feel comfortable to talk freely to someone that didn't know her or our situation.

It seemed she was gone all day. I was worried, but I knew she would be fine; she always was. She went to the beach after her therapy session to spend a little more time with herself. The therapist was very clear and told her she didn't have depression. She was grieving with the breakup we were going through.

Carly told me that she wanted to move on fast, get over us, and in doing so she couldn't be with me as a friend, it was too hard, it was a reminder, so she would rather not be with me at all.

She said she missed her mother so much too. We all did, but we knew she was around us too always. We could feel her presences, especially after Carly came back home. There were so many signs: chairs moving, curtains opening, sounds through the night, and when I would wake up, be woken up, I could feel someone standing over me. One time we were talking about her mum and we both went freezing cold instantly. It was such a bizarre experience. We knew it was Sarah, but we weren't scared. We were blessed to still feel her with us.

Carly planned to go back to the U.K. for a few weeks so she could decide what to do with her life now that we were not together, it would also give her time with her missed family. She said she did not know if she would come back, because if there was no us, then there was no life for her in Dubai.

Knowing that if she would go, she may never come back, was not easy.

To think it may be the last time I see her was a disturbing thought, play over. She set her alarm for the morning flight. She was leaving at 4 a.m. I was lying in bed wide awake, and could close my eyes, I just cuddled into her tightly. She was still questioning why I was not stopping her from going. She said she wanted me to want her. But I didn't really know what was going on myself. I told her that whatever she wants to do is up to her, I will support and not question. I told her she can have whatever she wants, it has nothing to do with what I want, the power of thought is so strong. I knew she has to believe it's available for her, and that she wants something so bad and she can't stop thinking about it, the opportunity will always present. It's just a matter of desire, faith, and belief.

The alarm went off, but we were already up. She got out of bed, dressed, stood over me as I lay there in bed, looking up at her, holding her hand. She kissed me on my cheek and said goodbye for possibly the last time.

Chapter 12
What Will Be Will Be

I woke up next morning to an empty pillow, but I was far from alone. I felt complete, surrounded with love. I felt myself, and I like being me.

I looked ahead, above me, to a picture on my wall which reminds me about my pursuit to my purpose.

> See your goals.
> Understand the obstacles.
> Create a positive mental picture.
> Clear your mind of self-doubt.
> Embrace the challenges.
> Stay on track.
> Show the world you can do it.

It's a picture of a man on the top of a mountain, with all the stars above him gazing down, standing proudly at the peak of the potential he was destined for.

The first letter, or the first word, in each motivating sentence spells **S-U-C-C-E-S-S.**

It was a meaningful gift from someone that means so much to me, and it has some deep meaning to its message. I was given it the day that I was facing my fears of public speaking, getting up on stage and confronting it in front of almost 1000 people. My wife she knew this was a big obstacle to overcome, which would be necessary for where I was heading.

She always did know how to say, or do, the right things at the right time to give me the confidence in my ability, and I will always love her deeply for that, even after death.

But how we start, will inevitably lead to how we finish, and that is no different from each day.

We should start the day the right way, to ensure to have the stride in our step to close it peacefully, with no regrets. Granted we cannot always choose where we wake, like we did not choose where we were born, but we can learn from it, understand not only how it happened, but why it happened, and it will deliver some truths we can walk by.

Waking up and reading the words on this picture, every morning as soon as I wake, this is one of the ways I ensure I am taking control of the day, from the second I am aware I am awake.

This reminds me of where I want to get to, what it will take, the recipe for success. This picture is also the last thing I look at before I close my eyes and drift into the dream land. It not only pumps fuel into my subconscious mind, driving my passion into a part of me I have less control of, but it also ensures I wake up with more understanding on how to navigate to turning my dream into my reality.

The day was going to be bright one, it was a good day to have a good day. I felt such confidence that every day that followed was going to be the same. Because I made one simple choice, I choose it to be.

Over the past few weeks, I had spent some quality time on my own, working on myself. Carly had been back in the U.K. for some time. We had been apart, separated, away from each other to spend time with the people that made us feel happy, although I know happiness is short lived, we should never seek to find happiness, we should seek the things that gives us moments of happiness. And for most it is finding their purpose and fulfilling their potential in that field.

I was happy on my own, I was feeling great. There was no pain, I was free from all the guilt I was feeling for so much of my life. I was not aware of any accusations, finger-pointing, or being judged, as I did not care for it. Only that it was helpful, and I accepted it as a part of life, as we are always being judged. I was at peace from the war in my mind, and I knew the battle I was in brought even more strength, for the next encounter with chaos, which will come. Because the line between chaos and order is an exceptionally fine one to walk. And fine was good reason, because it is the uncertainty that nudges us to stumble, but the lack of stability provides the needed lessons to complete the journey. If the path were a breeze, like waking through the park, there would be no opportunity for self-development, there would be no self.

While I was exploring ideas, and questioning the existence of everything, became more philosophical, Carly was with her loved ones sharing joy and laughter, feeling love, giving love and sharing it with everyone. The contrast between us both was quite different, but we are two completely different people, born in a different time, so it was understandable to me at least, but not so much for others.

Carly would share with them my new finding, as I would share with her, which was unintentionally creating a picture in their minds that I was losing my marbles. My sanity was questioned, my instability. This caused much concern, which was kind of nice and not really. You will be surprised how quickly you can respond defensively when you feel absolutely fine, better than ever, clear of your mindset, sharp with your thinking and your intelligence is downed on, and mistaking for mental health problems. But I understood me, I was on my side, and that was all I needed, all I could really ask for.

As there are dark forces lurking that were capable of the unimaginable, and if they sunk their teeth into you, you were bitten and poisoned with ill health, then there was only one way of seeing, and it was clear, it was a miserable fall. My father had experienced it, he wrote about it in his diary, he opened my eyes to the underworld, and taught me some lesson, to stay the hell away from that for God's sake.

He had met the Devil, and the Devil was hunting him down.

Because the Devil is no joke, everything you could ever imagine and worst. Your most feared nightmare itself would seem like a children's story, to pitiful existence opening that book would lead to.

I understood my father's language, the story behind what the eyes can see, it's of being an artist, and the gift presented by one. Passing the consciousness through a still object and communicating in this way years after it was expressed brings so much light of knowing. The expansion of my awareness form what such a thought can lead to, is a blessing from above, and one I will pass to another.

Piece by piece, the puzzle was complete, and I could make sense of it.

I could understand why my father was so desperate for help. Crying for a chance to think straight again, so he could learn more. Because he had so much more to learn. He knew, and I do, there was much, but he was focused on his aiming for the stars, distracted by his enemies which were distorting his reality.

My father was obsessed, as I am too. But he believed he was possessed.

Infected with an idea that his mind was being hijacked by an evil spirit.

He had become fearful of life, fearful of living. He fears not death but did not wish to die. The Devil was after him. There seemed to be no way out of this one for him, and he was willing to sacrifice his life for his beliefs, which he kind of did, as the day he discovered was the day he stood still and let his world collapse.

But what some may not believe is that, shortly before his life ended, he told someone close to the family that the Devil was after him and that he was going to die a horrible death in a fire. Which he then did in his own flat.

The diary

I want to be fast, but I must not make a show of it.

But I must wash my face.

And put on a cheerful atone.

If you do not want me to have the flat which I do want, then I will not have.

If I have been listening to Devil's people, forgive me.

When God plants a good seed in my heart, the Devil comes to take away that seed, and I can lose a little spiritual power which is a gift from God.

However, today I feel that in the last episode that the Devil has little power over me because I gladly admit to all my flaws, and humbly I keep calling God almighty the father and surrender to him because I know that I am not perfect and that only God is perfect and I know that all I need is his constant love and teaching to make me more acceptable, move more near to perfection in his sight.

Is it the beast that tells me to pluck out my left eye or is that your way of telling me not to on drugs?

Father, even if you wanted me to pluck out my eye to save me from going to hell, I have not enough.

But if you did want me to do it, then I would have to wait until I save enough money and have it to buy an operation. If this I must do as a repentance from kissing the beast. Please forgive me.

Dear Father, allow not the Devil to tempt me and misguide me and lead me astray from your will.

I know that the Devil can come through me, out of me.

Lord, free me from captivity.

Father, keep with me please the knowledge that all wrongdoing comes from the Devil and help me not to blame and individualize human being.

But give me the strength to try and connect a human if he/she makes error in yours sight.

Father, I know that there is a log in my own eye, so please keep me humble.

If you really desire for me to do something you know I do not have the strength to do it, which I am told this is not your will, please, then even if, as above, allow me time to do it in a civilized manner.

After my father's passing over, there were a lot of question marks hovering around his death. I had a few of my own, and more whilst reading the final few pages of his diary.

Why someone would go back into a flat of fire, he must known there was a risk of being burnt.

I even thought that maybe that was his way out of the hell he was in, running back into the fire, in hope that could only lead him to his savior.

Free from all mental torture he was facing.

Maybe he gave into what was chasing him and was called in.

I am not sure, even to this day, but I know the answers will someday come, and I have my faith, and my personal beliefs, that tell me all that is available is coming, and that I have to be prepared for it, so I should continue to work on myself. These have been embedded in me over years of experience.

My father had his own, one's that were there from his.

There was one seed planted in the mind of my father, that was manifesting over years, and I believe could have been the reason for all this confusion, but I don't think he was aware of how influential one incident could be on his decisions and actions. There was certainly no mentioning of it in the diary.

My mother told me years ago when I was a young boy, as she often told me stories of my dad, and she was too trying to steer on the right path.

My mum is a strong woman, with strong beliefs, she believes in life after death, and spirits of all kinds, good, and evil spirits.

She taught many stories that had so much meaning, never to play with fire or you will get burnt, type of stories.

She told me that they never had a lot of money coming in, she was looking after us, and my dad was an artist, which was not making a great deal.

So, he used to hustle, get by, they both did. One of the ways my father used to get a little extra cash would be to give blood, and get paid for doing it. There was a clinic where he would go, there were many other people there too, all just getting by. He started hanging around with the wrong crowd. One time they decided to do a Ouija board, a way of connecting with evil spirits and communicating.

There were five of them sitting around a wooden board with the alphabet A-Z in big letters around the top, and the numbers from 1-10 across the bottom, and off to one side, YES and NO, as well as END. In the center of the board there was an upside-down pint glass, where all five of them would put their fingers gently on.

It was like a board game, but a game you wished you had never played, as seeing and feeling an object move without the force of you would send shivers down your spine and be on your mind for, well, let's just say a long time, till forever.

They started by asking basic questions to see if the glass would start moving. YES and NO based questions, nothing specific, "Is there anyone on the other side?" The glass slid from the center to the word YES and back to center. "How many of us are here", which from what I am told, when you insult the intelligence of these spirits, they can get very angry if that is an emotion on the other side. The glass glided fast to the number 5.

After some time of going back and forth, by this time it is like their hands were glued, they had the choice but they were intrigued and thirsty for more.

They asked the spirit, "What do you want from us?"

The glass rapidly flew to the letter J, then to the letter O, in no time at all, then to H, N, spelling out the word 'JOHN'.

It kept going up and down through each letter of his name, faster and faster, with such speed and accuracy, stopping dead in the same position is it did seconds before, JOHN, JOHN, JOHN, it was screaming to them all.

My father freaked out, like any person would, he pulled his hand off the glass, but it kept furiously moving. They all pulled their hands off, but the glass kept spelling out the word JOHN, so John kicked the glass through the air until it met the ground it smashed on. He ran all the way home, petrified of what had just happened.

My mum said that this day his life started taking a downhill descent. And something tragic happened to all that played the game, all that danced with the Devil.

John ran away from the biggest fear in one's life, a fear that that he would eventually have to face.

He was never the same after that night. Paranoid, and afraid of what he knew was always there, but he never saw.

Everywhere he went, that shadow following, which you can only ignore for so long, until it blocks the light of others, and someone else addresses it to you.

My father needed help from someone that could see from a far, from above, to warn of potential outcomes form the doing and pitfalls to prepare for ahead.

He could have made better conscious decisions if there was a force nodding him forward, instead of pushing him back.

Like ones I have felt, the helping hand from other side, through the fabric that separates our reality and connects our beliefs.

There is a higher power, that is a fact, there is always something beyond our current capabilities. Because with more time, even we will be more capable in our doings.

To think there is no higher intelligence, would be to say that my life as we know it, has no more potential, and we know we have endless possibilities.

There is a constant battle between good and evil going on, you could call it God vs the Devil.

And to hear people get so motivated about the, so called 'fact' that there is no life after death, that there is not a place we evolve into after this living in this world is laughable.

Here's why, and what I know. Before the start of my conscious awakening, which happens when we are a few years old, I was a little boy, and before that I was just a baby. I did not even have a name. There was no world in your eyes, although I was clearly living in one, but not yet self-aware.

If we rewind to a few weeks before January the 8th 1987, the day I was born, I was just a fetus, living in a sack, that created the perfect environment to grow and adapt. I was fed information through a code, from outside whatever I was connected too, which I had no idea of. I was protected, and provided with the perfect balance of stress and comfort which helped me grow at the fastest, safest possible way.

Which by the way was made up of mostly water, and I was upside down, upright, spinning, moving, but I also had no idea at all.

Now, I could argue, by definition, there is a lot of similarities to the world I live in now, and if I get deep into my way of thinking, a lot more than what I have presented.

Now, let's rewind before that, I was in another world like surrounding, I was a sperm, traveling to my purpose driving destination, one I felt compelled to reach. At this level even my way of thinking was as simple as a nucleus delivering information to the mitochondria to create an action.

Before I made it that far to the womb to start the biggest journey of my life, at that point, I was in a different world like surrounding. I was a sperm in the testicles of another, not yet entered the womb.

We could keep going back further and further, right to the creation of the first ever cell on this world, and the first spark of light that moved into the cosmos.

Who would have thought there was so many tiers of evolution to get to the point we are now. And we know that to the universe is moving forward, forever expanding. We are the same material, we are moving into the direction we are being pulled towards, preparing for the birthed into something a lot bigger, with more understanding than we have now.

My beliefs come from my personal findings, and I have found, that even in this life itself, my world has changed around me, I have evolved and adapted, I am preparing for the next phase in my soul's journey through time.

My view of this existence is so different from before.

The journey I have been on, one that I can look back and see, has taught me so much about life, and connecting to others.

I have experienced new pain, my heartbreaking and the heartache that emerged. I have traveled to destinations that many of the richest on this planet have yet to discover. I have been at the bottom of a dark, cold and lonely staircase, as well as at the top of the world sharing the experience with so many that exchanged their gratitude. By digging deep within myself, I found answers to questions I was brave enough to ask.

And my biggest realization is that we are connected to each other, to everything, we are all in control of whatever we desire.

We are the artists painting the world that is molded around our point of attention.

And through my life's lessons, and the lessons my father taught me, I understand a lot more.

I was in and how my feelings toward my wife started to fade as I took less notice of her charm.

It's because I wanted more support than what my wife was giving. I wanted someone to see me for who I was and not judge me on the decisions I was making. I didn't want to feel the need to seek acceptance from others, but the one that was the least accepting was always me. I wanted to connect with higher realms, and disconnect with those that was less encouraging.

I wanted to spend time with someone that shared the same passion for life and my chosen path. I was much aware of the power of thought, as I was, someone just like me, but the only person just like me is me.

There was a gap where my wife once stood, which challenged me to build a bridge and a deeper relationship with the person I wanted to become. It was written in the stars from long before my arrival and long before our eyes met.

We are in control; it is our choice. But we are not always aware of that, I was not. I was a fool to my own way of thinking, but I love myself for that, actions made me a better person to not just me, but all around, which is my everything.

I have finally realized, that all the practices I have been preaching, I have been practicing without even knowing.

Believe to achieve, ask and you shall receive.

I wanted to know more about my father, his battles, his story, and why he went back into the fire, what he was going through at that time in his life, whether he was going mad or not, and then came his diary with all of the above to uncover.

I really wanted to overcome my fear and to speak onstage in front of thousands of people, delivering an inspiring message, and there was the opportunity waiting for me to grab.

I dreamed of living in a beautiful country that everyone talked about, with spectacular views, luscious beaches, likeminded people to help me grow, and I am now living in Dubai, the best place in the world.

I wanted to change the way I looked, and other people saw me. I wanted to use my body to change the way I felt. I found bodybuilding. I became a champion and a role model for many people that are battling their own negative thoughts about the way they look.

Whatever we desire we can have. If we can see it in our mind, we can have it in our life. We just need to believe it's coming, and be smart enough to recognize the opportunities it brings.

We are the writers, the directors, the actors, and the producers in our own movie we call life. It really is up to us. We have a choice every day. We can choose to be happy while being alive or choose to be sad waiting to die, it is that simple.

Unfortunately, my father believed he was being chased by the devil and that he was going to die in a fire. It is that belief that shifted his focus and all his attention that led to exactly that. He created his own reality, one that would lead him to an early grave, a grave he was not aware he was digging long before his body laid in it.

But in doing so, he created a legacy, he taught me so many lessons from his own. If it wasn't for his life ending the way it did, my life would not be the way it is.

If I had not read the diary, I would not have asked for help to avoid going down a similar road he went. I wouldn't have met the people that helped me connect and see the truth within.

I wouldn't have understood God, spoke to him and been taught that everything has a meaning, and everything is about timing.

There were many times I thought I was going mad, hearing voices in my mind, like my father described too, that persuaded choices that were not aligned with the way I was once wired.

I found hard to explain at first, but that was my lack of maturity, now it's so simple and it has always been, just hard to see when you are not looking.

God is me, I am God, and God lives in us all; we are all connected. I was always guiding me too. Guiding me from above, my higher self. Planting messages in my path and encouraging me to take the best route whilst pulling me towards my soul's purpose.

And we are all spiritually connected to these cords that guide our souls and unite us in this existence that will last forever. We have the capability to experience multiple realities, all of which we can choose, it is a matter of mindset which allows us to travel.

Our intuition, the whispers, are from my own source of energy communicating down through layers of existences, tweaking the cords that steered us.

The expansion of the universe and the collapsing of everything has been, is, and will always be. Yin Yang, chaos and order, the aim is to find the fine line in between, that is the aim of everything, as that is where the quickest path to eternal progression lays.

Chapter 13
The Passing of Ages

Carly would be soon returning to Dubai, and I wondered what she would say of my new way of thinking, as we had not talked much over the last few weeks. I also wondered what I would think about what she had to say.

I was not sure whether she would be moving back in with me or moving out, as she did not state. I did not know if she was staying in Dubai or moving to Australia, because the last time she was with me, she said she may.

Although the future of our relationship was uncertain, I was certain we would be better people, we would be stronger, and happier than we ever imagined we could be. I knew that the time apart would allow us both to find ourselves and to find our way onto the path to becoming complete, as the one we were on were taking us further from it. I knew I was going to make it to the top of whatever mountain I climbed. My business would become a globally recognized brand. I had visions of standing in large stages, speaking from many platforms, to motivate and inspire thousands. And I believed in doing so my family would be so proud, it would make me cry only happy tears, no pain, or regret. And I knew my father was eternally proud of me. I made sense of interaction and everyone I had met along my way. I understand that there were always spiritual guides sent from above, guiding me, teaching me, and looking out for me, as I made my way through the struggled times.

I believed that my father wrote the diary for me to read. Which helped me overcome many loses and see them as opportunities to learn from.

I believed that there was no coincidence, everything falls the way it is meant to land, and picked up by the hand that is meant to receive it, at precisely the right time.

I was so confident, I knew what I wanted, understand what it was going to take, and I accepted that there would need to be sacrifices made, and the bigger the sacrifice often leads to the biggest reward.

I could also see that for many years, more so the last few months, I was not giving my relationship the attention it deserved, I was not giving to my wife.

I was so fixated on fixing me, at first my body, which was driven by my ego, my reputation, which was too. The fixing the cracks in my personality, by crushing everything I was, so I had the chance to start all from scratch and fix it right.

But know I was healed, I was solid, I was whole again, I was unbreakable, and it was the right time to switch my focus and attention. It was time to let someone back in, and expand upon the awareness of the doing, and the doing of the work.

But I was still fully committed to my goals, and that was not going to change, no one was going to change myself if it was not aligned with my work, which is my life.

I was in the heart of creation, one that the artist will live within. Pass on to my children and the children of them.

I booked a weekend away on the same day Carly was landing in Dubai, down in Abu Dhabi. I thought it would be better to get away for a few days, to ensure there were no distractions and no memories of negative emotions.

The plan was to spend two full days together. I was interested to see how we would get on, how the conversation would flow, or sink, after all it a while since we had been this close and we were both different people, different from each other and from who we were.

By the time we arrived at the hotel, I knew I would know what was meant to be.

Someone once told me a story that made so much sense to me when she did.

She told me that one day there was a successful middle-aged woman on her Yacht, just peacefully drifting out in the middle of the sea, enjoying the sun.

The women had great fortune. She was a believer in God, and devoted her life in the helping of others.

God was kind to this woman in return, he gave her everything she could desire and more.

Her trust, and faith were so stronger, and stronger than any glue she used to fix the others her broken relationships.

The women noticed there was water in the lower deck. But she did not worry, it was not too much of a concern. So, she went back up to sunbath.

After some time, she noticed there was a lot more, and quickly realized that she could be in a little trouble. But again, she did not panic, as she believed her life would be long, as she had trust in God to save her.

With that another yacht came by, close enough for the women to call out, and ask for a helping hand, but that she didn't, she had too much pride, and believed that she was safe, and God would save her.

Some more time went passed, and the entire lower deck was filled with water. A fishing boat came from nowhere with an old man on board. Accompanied by a few buckets of dead fish, and a dirty old net. The man could see there was a need for help, he called out and asked if she wanted to come on board. The women said that she was fine, and that someone else is on the way, she was all the help she needs.

The boat went past, and the yacht continues to sink.

The women was now in a little panic, stress, but soon followed with a little smile, as she knew her God would come to save her.

But not much time after, she started to lose hope.

Suddenly a small boat with an even older man on there, threw her a rope and shouted, "CLIMB ON LADY"!

She told the man the same, that she was waiting for someone, and he will be here any minute. So, the boat went on. As it did the yacht sunk, and she was paddling for her life, praying to God, asking him to save her.

It got too much, she did not have the stamina, she went down, and took her last breath.

She opened her eyes and she was at the gates of heaven.

She was furious; she was annoyed; she was confused.

She waited for a short time, as the emotions built ready to throw them at whoever she would meet.

God appeared, "you said you were going to save me. I trusted you. I believed in you. I sacrificed my life for you, and you let me down!" She blurted out.

God looked at the woman in the eyes and said calmly, "I sent you three boats, my dear. I tried to save you."

The women dropped to her knees and begged him for his forgiveness in not being blinded to her own ignorance.

There is a lot of meaning and messages in this story.

When you believe in something so much, it will come, but you must take notice to the signs, and look a little deeper. Which can be hard, especially when you are living in the thoughts of the future. You will not only get the opportunity if you let it pass, you often only get one, you are lucky if you get more, and stupid if you ignore.

Thank you, Dr. Dawn, it made so much sense, not just in my personal life but in the lives of those around me. It sparked questions with no answered needed, like;

Why would someone keep giving if we are not appreciating?

Why would someone stay with you if you don't show them, you wanted them to stay?

Why would someone give you all their love if you are not giving yours to them?

There was much confusion before, but now it's so plain to see.

There is deep meaning behind the messages in the diary, which has shown to be a bridge for connection between two dimensions, Earth and astral plane.

I have always been guided from above. My father has always been there; he is there now. We are all connected from the birth of existence, and forever after. United to a flow of something that's thicker than blood, threaded together, streaming from the source of everything.

We have with the ability to see the world we desire through our minds eye, shape it, attract it, and embody it.

The door opens, unexpected but almost predictable.

Something was different.

She was glowing from inside.

She had dyed her hair blue and was wearing a nose ring she could not hide.

There was a new tattoo on her sleeve, which matched her new glow.

It was reminder of places she had been, the ones that taught her to grow.

The struggles she faced, she now looked at and smiled.

She was the girl the cocoon, living in fear and pain, away from the world is where she cried.

Until the day came, that she had no shame, regret, only pride.

The day she broke through the shell, spread the wings from her side.

Some people worried; she would die if she fell.

But I knew from the beginning, that she could fly well.

For she is a Divine spirit, that I could always tell.

Now she has awakened, she flies forward into a confident glide.

For the truth of knowing will shine through her to the people that need it, the light will find.

The butterfly tattoo on her arm represents the journey to her, but I see the wings she spreads as far more.

A gift from above that was sent for me that day, the love of an angel and the message that says.

Through the world we travel, lows and highs, I will lift you up, or your darkest days.

I will carry you far beyond the highest skies, to a place we have not yet seen.

Where we have touched hands many times, more in we have in our dreams, as from this day forward, we are together, bathing in love streams.

There is a story that goes well with the butterfly, that I would like to share.

One day a man was passing by a butterfly about to come to life.

It was handing from a tree, struggling to break free.

From that day, I started writing in my own diary, mostly after I came out of deep meditation sessions.

I knew it would be helpful for me in the moment, and potentially future moments.

My Diary

Today I connected with my higher self, but little did I know, we already met before.

Today I was reintroduced, and I remembered.

My first encounter was in a dream a few weeks back. The connection was so powerful, it woke me out of a deep sleep. Even back then, I knew it meant something, but I did not know what it was or what it was for.

As usual, my conscious mind filled in the blanks.

I knew it wasn't a thought of my own. It was so much deeper than anything I had ever experienced. It was a connection with the Divine source, a spiritual engagement that was bonded long before, one that was meant to lead to a ceremony, the awakening of one's self.

This time it was during this morning's meditation practice. I had a very brief but beautifully powerful interaction with my true guider.

Although it was more intense than any experience I have ever felt in my life, it was very short-lived, but that didn't matter, because it was enough to understand the power from within, the cosmic energy it carries, the light from about, from everything there was, is, and will be.

The Divine source, my higher self, my spirit, passed through codes of wisdom, touching me with an orgasmic bliss of happiness and the gift of seeing what was before or beneath this experience, gifting me with a map to where the lock was and the key by going deep inside, finding one's true essence and unlocking it.

What was quite misleading by everything before this point was how I thought I was fueled by masculinity, manpower, but the spirit I met with today was feminine.

She came with such authority but encouraging way that allowed me to comfortably surrender to her, submit, and silence my thoughts, my defense, my fear, and my will to move, to be still and absorb, to be full alert and aware of the opportunity that will lead to the guidance from above toward my chosen path. The path that was chosen long before my existence of this life, or at least in this life form.

She gave me confidence. She felt like someone I knew. Mother Earth, the nature that has always supported me, my God, guardian angel, the one that only has the best intentions for me and for everything around me.

As the words find paper whilst I document my experienced moments after I had it, my awareness has been brought to a few experiences I have had this week, this month, and even this year. I am reminded how certain spiritual beings, family, friends, mentors, leaders, partners, followers, and the messages I have received are all from above, placed here for me so I can move forward. They are all part of the bigger picture, as I am too.

I am unsure they even know their role and the predicted impact they have had on my life, that they were meant to have, like the impact I had on theirs was all for the better of their existence, for all of ours. Collectively we have achieved so much together. We are a massive team, a network or vibration that's driving us all forward, individually on a small scale but collectively on a big one.

I am blessed with my understanding as well as everything I received from above. The seeds they planted inside my thoughts that bedded in my subconscious mind, which were nourished until they grew, until they poked through the cracks and to the surface so I could benefit from them today.

All the breadcrumbs that lead to here are so easy to see when I look back now, leading me into acceptance and to allow the guidance from a figure from above.

I realize that there have been many of the same gestures or persuading whispers that were there to bring me to this point, this day, today. But, like many times in my life, I refused to listen. I rebelled when I heard due to my masculine ego. Even my ego I now know was needed to build the appreciation and respect I have for the opposite sex, which I now know is also just a label to describe one's output, but within we are all the same, we are one.

By understanding the pattern in the path, I walked through, that I stumbled across by no will of my own, it was only a matter of time before I met, before we met, and it would be so clear. The confidence, the knowledge, the reassurance I have obtained through, which tested me but evolved my awareness and allowed me to see that it really is true. Everything is timing, and everything is positioned perfectly in place at precisely the right time in order to progress, in order to grow.

I recognize that my human mind, my intelligence, my emotions, my physical limitations are all necessary to build my character for the journey that lies ahead. The struggles I faced, fears I faced, pain I suffered with, the thoughts I battled with, and the lessons I was tested during, were all needed to force the transition, transformation, and transcendence.

It's the mind that tends to pull us back to the ignorant idea that this three-dimensional world is all there is, and any topic that seems a little extraordinary, or episodes in our life that seem so aligned with our thoughts and predictions are nothing more than coincidences, which not only keep us comfortable, stable, safe, sometimes grounded, but also humbled too, which is a nice life to live.

But when we let our strength, faith, belief quickly override these ideas of self-doubt and doubt in generic, this will lead to not a nice life but a spectacular one with endless possibilities.

It's hard to hear our intuition or pay attention to, because it's deep. It whispers. The voice comes from our guided angels, guiding us to where we are meant to be, if we let them in and let them take us.

I have chosen to open my heart up. It was shielded for a while, but now I am carried to my highest desires, to my destiny.

Today I am blessed and thankful, excited and also calm, as I move forward into the guided future of myself. One that will lead the way for those that choose to listen, to follow their intuition and their whispers. To those that see me as everything I am. I am an extension of themselves living in their world, there for a purpose, to help them move in the positive direction they are meant to be, and, in return, they are silently doing the same for me. To plant the fruitful seeds of awareness and curiosity to how one is able to stay focused, engaged, achieve such heights considering his story and where he started. Then sit back, watch them flourish, blossom, evolve into the buttery life they're *meant to be, watch them spread their wings and fly.*

This is my calling, my purpose, this is my gift and what I am gifted with today.

My father's diary

Yesterday, wisdom showed a certain truth, only I was not wise enough to comprehend her.

Her splendor is so beautiful and enriching in life, if only my wits were sharper to see her then, I would have to make the mistake, because she always comes to rescue me before I fall and play the fool, the idiot, but I am often too slow.

Today is November the 2nd, 2019. A new day. A new chapter in my life and the lives around me. Today is a new beginning, the rebirth of two once-lost souls that found their way back together. Today is the renewal of my vows, the commitment I promised to keep as I started the journey of 'We'.

Everything that has passed, was to bring us to this point right here and right now.

I set the mood, prepared the stage for the curtain to drop and reveal the mystery behind it. We are sharing a bottle of wine, reminiscing on our lives. Where we were, where it took us, and how far we have traveled.

I sit in the air of outdoors, on the soft chair that comforts me. And I just stare out from this perfectly situated balcony that casts its glare over the calm and clear Gulf Sea. The ripples from the ocean drift peacefully toward me from as far as I can see.

My surrounding is spacious, but its filled, I am not alone and I am thrilled. I haven't been for some time. Feeling the presence of another as usual, but one that is a part of me. In this moment and all that follows, I am always connected. Its force is so strong, it engaged us from our tangled self. Today is a special day. It has been for long back. It symbolizes the life of something unique, a gift from an angel sent from above, and the opportunity to experience unconditional love.

Today is the anniversary of my wedding day five years ago. It is also the anniversary of the first date I went on with my wife six years before that.

We had so many great times together and visited places many only dream to go. So many amazing experiences, unforgettable memories, adventurous stories to tell, wrapped in a book of love, ready to be passed to others.

I am stronger now, like I knew I would be. She is too, just as I knew she would be. I accept everything for what it is and how it is meant to be. I trust my intuition. No longer second-guessing decisions. The future in our marriage was far from certain less than six months ago, but I knew the future of our friendship would certainly clear. I held on to my faith, it was the only thing that kept me going. I knew we would get through and not only that, be better. We needed time apart, and had to break the bond to be there, which was hard.

That was the only way for us both to receive, adapt, evolve, and learn from. I felt it in the depths of my core, deep in my heart. It took breaking to release it and to realize it.

This day that reminds us of the past and we smile remembering the good times and not the bad. We kept our relationship alive; we saw each other for the gifts of life we were, the extension of our souls' in the repetitive time lapse journey it goes through.

Today I am incredibly blessed. I am privileged to have shared this moment with her.

The future is even brighter than the present and the present is far brighter than the past.

I know she will be the best mum to a beautiful child that will grow up as loving as her, a star that will shine just like her.

My only wish, which I have a lot of hope for, is that I will get the chance to pass my wisdom through many stories I am excited to tell.

I pray I get the chance to teach by creating lessons. Examples of the mistakes I have made, and how to move on from.

Today I promise to live by, and for the same principles as I was willing to sacrifice my marriage for and the relationships that were forged.

Which was to better my life, to better the lives of others.

I take a sweet sip on the crisp wine in my hand, look up, take a breath in whilst the sunset seems to rest, and I relax my expression.

I am in heaven, touched by an angel, injected with pure love.

I reach for my pocket, and I take to one knee. I look at her and I promise to love, care, cherish, and to stay faithful to her.

I promise to stay connected through thick and thin, through the highs and the low, and promise to always give my everything to her, as she is everything to me.

I open a box to an 18-carat white-gold ring. It faces 12 diamonds that farm its beauty. Each diamond represents every year we have been through, and I am confident we will make it through the coming year.

She looks stunning, all I can do is look. Her eyes are tearing up, but this time with happy emotions. I place the ring on her finger, position it in front of her wedding ring that is in front of the ring her mum passed to her before she passed.

Soon after we planned to travel to America, from L.A. to Las Vegas, and San Francisco.

We discussed revisiting where we got married and dinning at the top-of-the-world restaurant as the landscape of the city turned into a skylight.

We discussed how we had to do all the traveling sooner rather than later, as we were expecting a baby. Clark J.K. Williams, a son of my own. J.K after John Kaler.

My son will become my best student, my proudest piece of art. I will teach him right from wrong, lead him into the right direction. Show him the rewards desire, discipline, and the determination by leading by an example. I will encourage him to discover within his self. I will help him understand the value of life and the meaning of his existence. I will tell him stories of the benefits ~~to~~ of knowing self, and why thy shall steer towards it.

The uniqueness of women, and how precisions they are.

I will remind him of his mum, of my mum, and how to find the right mum.

And encourage him to open up, express himself, and show others how to do the same.

I will show him love, by giving him so much. Help him find his passion, realize his potential, and pursue his purpose, even if it is not aligned with everyone else.

And let him discover that his probability of his dreams and goals coming true or not depends on the mindset.

I ensure I do not cast a shadow of guilt, and that his life was taking course well before mine even began. And that he was coming anyway, I was just lucky enough to be a part of it.

I will inspire him to listen to his inner voice, his intuition, and look within to seek.

I will motivate him to strive to the top, then reach back and pull others with him.

Stay to true to his faith and to trust is doing.

I will tell him about his dad, and my dad. Stories of bravery and heroic tales.

And that any bright morning, can shine light, through any dark day.

As well as tell him to look closely at every cloud of doubt, and he will see that it has a silver lining.

But the biggest gift of realization I can share with him is that his grandfather wrote a diary, that was a document of emotions. It was kept for his dad, until the time was right. When his dad read it, it steered his path, and kept him on the straight and narrow, instead of falling into a destructive past.

The diary spoke to his dad, in a way only words can describe, and said the right words, when they were needed the most.

The reading of the shared diary sparked the idea to write a book to share.

With the inspiration to inspire and lead one from despair.

The diary was written to be read by his son, as was the book, but that son was you.

This is a story for you, for when you are at the age you feel ready, at a time in your life you feel, like I was felt, and need that little help.

I call this the passing of ages, when your path crosses mine, for that will be the time, you need the guide from above, in the form of words written by my hand.

Clark. I love you. I always have, even before you were here.

I am so proud of you.

You are a gift that helped so many of us make it to the other side.

You were my light, that brightens my day, you were the life I dreamt of and prayed.

You will grow up to be amazing.

I know this even before your life has begun.

You are greatness.

And this book will inspire you to document your story, in whatever form you choose, so you too can pass it on to your son.

As with great power comes great responsibility, and once you know, you know.

This is my message to you I will leave my print on.

Below is a poem I wrote to my father on Father's Day in 2016, a few weeks before we moved to America to start on our journey overseas.

What it would lead to, I had no idea, but I was excited, driven, and I was eager.

Dear dad

Although you past many years ago.

I feel you near everywhere I go.

Your life was dedicated to a passion you possessed.

Chasing your ambitions and dreams in life for success.

This has been the driving force of me and our team.

You have inspired me to do the same, I am excited and keen.

To be the best person, friend, son, husband, bodybuilder, brother, professional, leader, and the man I can be.

To live a life for the both of us that was taken from not just you but me.

Now we are the same age as you were when you left.

Although your time on earth has come to a stand.

Like in a relay, I have been waiting for your hand.

To take the torch and carry it through the next phase, the new age and new land.

I told you before, I will live my life loud, to the fullest, never moan, complain, feel sorry for myself, always be generous and kind.

I will look after the people around us in hope to obtain a life you wanted, in hope to do you proud.

Love you, Dad, and I feel you more than ever. In the next chapter of my life, we will live together.

Life may seem short and a bumpy ride, but thanks to you I am strong, confident, powerful, never afraid to back down or hide.

I have taken the wheel and the bull by the horns to ride through the storm, foot down, to the clear path, I will get us both home.

Happy Father's Day.

Thanks for being there even if it seems you are not. Your love and encouragement are felt and I feel it a lot.

x x x x x x x x x x x x x x x x x x x x x x x

Dad, you have given me the fire to start my heart.

The title to this book you gave, and it helped me to write it from the start.

START A FIRE
In Your Heart

John Kaler